Classical
Philosophy
IN A
NUTSHELL

Classical Philosophy
IN A NUTSHELL

Michael Moore

ARCTURUS

ARCTURUS

This edition published in 2018 by Arcturus Publishing Limited
26/27 Bickels Yard, 151–153 Bermondsey Street,
London SE1 3HA

Copyright © Arcturus Holdings Limited

ISBN: 978-1-78828-371-7
AD006045UK

Printed in China

Contents

Introduction

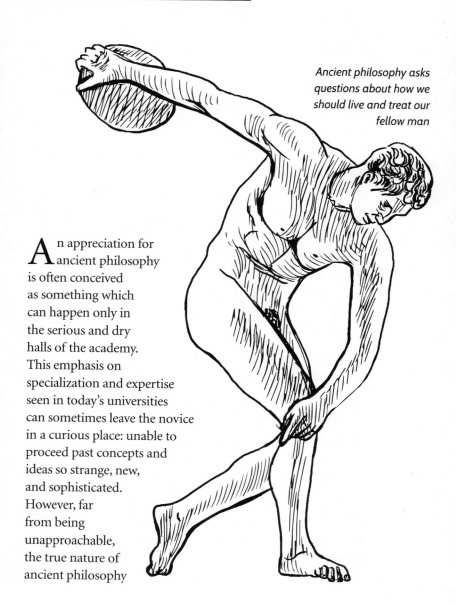

Ancient philosophy asks questions about how we should live and treat our fellow man

An appreciation for ancient philosophy is often conceived as something which can happen only in the serious and dry halls of the academy. This emphasis on specialization and expertise seen in today's universities can sometimes leave the novice in a curious place: unable to proceed past concepts and ideas so strange, new, and sophisticated. However, far from being unapproachable, the true nature of ancient philosophy

Socrates was said to have brought philosophy down from the heavens

is a way of thinking which is entirely human and mundane at its core. It is an expression of those human concerns which we all have, whether we are a pauper or queen, rich or poor, young or old. Ancient philosophy asks about what is real, what we as human animals are, whether and what a soul is. It asks about how we are to live, what our purpose in life is, and how we are to treat our fellow humans. It asks about how we are to think, whether we are to trust our senses, how it is that we can come to believe and justify our beliefs. These concerns are the common coin of humanity, asked and answered in many cultures and in different ways.

This book seeks to give you a sympathetic first approach to ancient philosophy understood in this humanistic light. Just as Socrates was said to have taken philosophy down from the heavens and delivered it to earth, so this book seeks to simplify, summarize and expound ancient philosophy. As such the purpose of this book is ideally as an entry point for further study. After a broad exposure to many different thinkers and traditions, the reader should feel comfortable wading out into deeper waters and exploring both more and more deeply the works of

Philosophers like Plato created a whole empire of ideas to be explored

philosophers they have been introduced to here. When you have finished the book, this volume will still serve as a ready refresher or as a quick reference for dates, ideas, or technical words. Additionally, keep in mind that the ideas of the philosophers expressed here were often chosen for their influence, fame or sometimes even for their controversiality. This is not a concession that these ideas are somehow unrepresentative of a given philosopher, rather it is an acknowledgment that, for whatever reason, certain beliefs of a given philosopher have had more general interest than others.

In the spirit of the 'In a Nutshell' series, comprehensiveness can never be expected either in the examination of a single philosopher nor in the scope of representative philosophers. In light of this confession, some philosophers simply could not be included among those chosen. Nevertheless, no other book can give such a concise overview of so many philosophers in a readily accessible book. Each chapter can be read in a sitting, each chapter is self-contained without any prior knowledge needed, and throughout each chapter are illustrations, charts and diagrams designed to clearly explain or exemplify the ideas found within. At the end of each chapter is a summary, useful as a concise overview and an aid to clear retention. A helpful glossary has also been included, for reference or perusal.

As I just mentioned, due to the scope of the material, some chapters simply could not give as comprehensive a picture of a given philosopher. Keeping this in mind is important for further self-study: whereas for more minor philosophers, such as Anaximander, a chapter approaches a general map of the land, for someone like Plato, his chapter can merely give you the boundaries of his philosophical empire. To know the scope of his philosophy, you are going to have to do a lot of legwork exploring his vast corpus. It is in cases such as this that a given chapter in this book shows itself to be more evidently non-comprehensive, but this should be understood for every chapter.

Because the chapters each have summaries, this may in fact be the best place to start for either comprehension or curiosity. That is, you may want to get an overview as an aid to understanding, or you may want to survey the ideas of the summary to see if they appeal to your interests, or if another chapter's philosopher is more appealing. In addition to the summaries, there are illustrations, which always have a reference in the text in some way. This means that the illustration is perhaps best understood if both the illustration and its explanatory text are taken in tandem.

Lastly, there are two charts illustrating relations among philosophers. One of these concerns the teacher and student relationships; the other, the various schools or sects of philosophy. These too should be referenced upon the completion of chapters. Not only does it help to clarify philosophical influence, or to emphasize dogmatic agreement or disagreement, it also identifies how all thinkers, including ourselves, are never entirely free from what our predecessors thought and believed.

Philosophers' Family Trees

These represent relationships of influence between philosphers other than those of teacher/student, with the possible exception of Cleanthes and Alcmaeon.

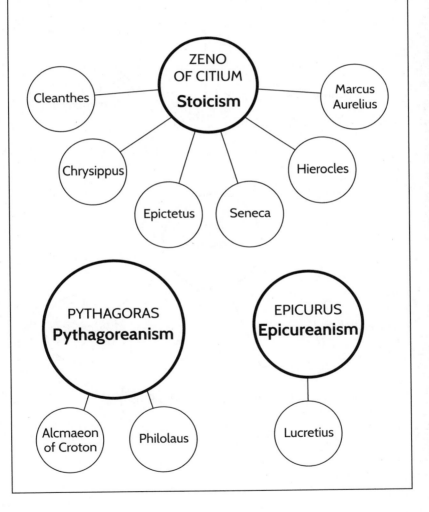

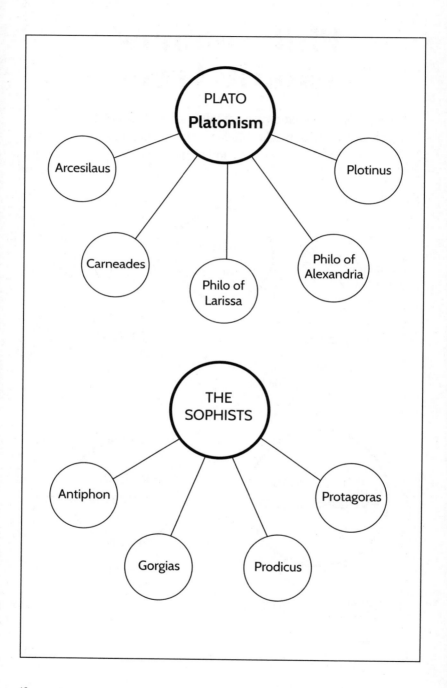

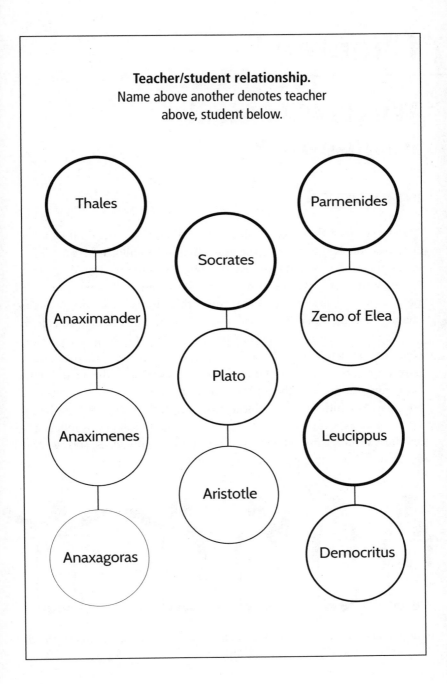

Teacher/student relationship.
Name above another denotes teacher
above, student below.

Thales

Anaximander

Anaximenes

Anaxagoras

Socrates

Plato

Aristotle

Parmenides

Zeno of Elea

Leucippus

Democritus

Chapter 1

What is Classical Philosophy?

INTRODUCTION

In the spirit of the 'In a Nutshell' series, *What is Classical Philosophy?* gives a concise overview of the most significant philosophers from the classical period in a readily accessible book. The philosophers of ancient Greece and Rome are vast in number and exceptionally varied in their range of ideas. This book provides you with an introduction to the main characters in the story of classical philosophy and their fascinating ideas.

The book begins with Thales, and concludes with Plotinus, a period covering the better part of 1000 years. There are twenty chapters, each covering one or more important figures in the classical tradition. It should also be mentioned that the topic of classical philosophy can be a difficult and therefore intimidating subject. However, the subject need not be so. Often mere exposure to the ideas presented in classical philosophers has an effect on the comprehension of the reader. Many ideas, strange and exotic on their first appearance, will soon become familiar.

Greek and Roman thinkers debated a range of subjects that they often categorized as ethics, logic and physics

Classical philosophy, for the purpose of this book, is simply the philosophers and philosophical schools that existed in the ancient Greek- and Latin-speaking worlds. Plato and Aristotle observed that philosophy begins in wonder, and it was wonder at the natural world that prompted the first philosophers to begin speculation about the constitution of the physical world. When we add the study of ethics and logic to this interest in nature, we get a threefold understanding of philosophy in the ancient world: ethics, logic and physics, which is how many classical philosophers divided philosophy. The ancient understanding of ethics, logic and physics, however, is different from that of the contemporary world. In classical philosophy almost the entire range of human life, familiar to the ancient as well as modern person, is examined and explained. Often in the exploration of these topics further claims are advocated, about how to live and how we do or ought to think. Classical philosophy can be thought of as something like a method, not necessarily defined by a set of rules, but rather by an attitude committed to seek out explanation, truth and meaning using all the rich resources of the human mind.

Classical philosophy is a subject taught academically throughout the West, often beginning with Socrates and Plato. Although Socrates and his student, Plato, do indeed begin a shift in philosophy, it is more intellectually fruitful to begin with the philosophers who preceded them. These so-called Presocratics not only set the stage for the kinds of questions and interests that follow in later eras, but they advocated views which were simultaneously fiercely defended and adamantly opposed. It is in the light of these debates that the later philosophers make their intellectual contribution. Thus, Plato adapts Heraclitus' theory of flux to his own theory of knowledge. The sophists look at the long history of bickering philosophers, observe the difficulty of coming to certain conclusions, and decide to focus on the teaching of argumentation. The sceptics, with similar information, decide that we should withhold from having opinions. Aristotle directly contradicts his master, Plato, in many areas, including, significantly, his political and ethical theory.

Classical philosophy can be a difficult and intimidating subject; however, it need not be so. Often mere exposure to the ideas present-ed by classical philosophers has an effect on the comprehension of the

Classical philosophy as a subject often begins with Socrates, but a whole range of influential 'Presocratics' came before with their own unique and insightful ideas

reader. For instance, it may sound odd to hear that Aristotle thinks that someone must be virtuous in order to live a happy life. We may immediately bring to mind examples of several 20th-century despots and dictators who were surely 'happy' while living a life characterized by wickedness, indulgence, injustice and other odious behaviours. Yet on further reflection it is not hard to sympathize with Aristotle's belief that in order to be truly happy one has to live a life in accordance with the virtues. At least we feel that if one is a moral wretch, one *should* be miserable and unhappy.

As one encounters classical philosophy, or any philosophy for that matter, it is important that modern conceptions associated with the term 'debate' or 'argumentation' be kept in check. That is, we tend to think of differing opinions as the manifestations of different personalities bickering. In the examination of philosophers from the past, however, such a perception is not only misguided but also misguiding. Classical philosophers disagreed strongly with each other, but it was almost always about something, never about someone. This is to say that differing opinions focused on issues, even if parochial prejudice sometimes did intrude into these disputes. Likewise, if we do not have an appreciative respect for the philosophers themselves, their arguments can slip our understanding. It is hard, for example, to take seriously the views of some Presocratics who claim the sun is a bowl of fire or the Socratic belief that no one willingly does evil. But it is precisely a type of open-mindedness to these ideas that makes them understandable. If we continually ask ourselves, '*Why* was this believed?' we can more easily understand with a sympathetic mind. If, on the other hand, we go looking for the absurdity in a strange idea, we are sure to find it there. To contemporary eyes, it is, after all, a strange idea.

One approach to the history of philosophy up to the time of Aristotle was to explain philosophy as a long search for one or more principles by which to explain the existence of the world. This trajectory was fixed by Thales' conception of the primary principle as water, and later philosophers, for better or for worse, continued with this project, offering their own candidate instead of water. Anaximander offered the boundless, Anaximenes offered air, Empedocles the four elements and strife/love, and Parmenides the unity of the One. There were others, of course, but these examples are sufficient to demonstrate a shared goal and a commitment to a type of explanation that would fit with the purposes of that goal. To be sure it was nothing like modern science, where progress, accumulation and consensus create new knowledge. No person or idea, for example, could stand in as an explanatory principle for the universe. The cosmic principle had to be something at least nominally physical, in order to explain the physical universe, and impersonal, to explain the material makeup of things. Thus, although not necessarily openly collaborative, there is a sense that classical philosophy was a socially organized enquiry.

In addition to shared goals, there were often shared assumptions. Many of the disputes when it came to how one should live nevertheless arose in the context of a common culture. For example, many Greek philosophers took it for granted that there were four chief virtues: wisdom, courage, temperance and justice, and that happiness (*eudaimonia*) was the chief goal of human living. Many also believed that living in accordance with nature, since nature provides a guide for us, was a rule we simply had to adopt. The problem, of course, was in what sense is something in 'accordance with nature'? It is difficult to say if ancient Greeks, for example, were more on the same page among themselves than contemporary philosophers are nowadays. With thousands of years of opinions from which to pick it is perhaps understandable that modern philosophers have many considered and differing opinions on all manner of topics. However, it is noteworthy to observe as an example that Socrates, as iconoclastic as he was, did not fundamentally challenge the existence of the gods in his courtroom defence, but rather contested the picture of the gods as conceived by the populace. At any rate, shared cultural, ideological and theological beliefs formed the ground for dispute in the ancient world to a degree often underappreciated.

Literary Background

The fledgling discipline of philosophy was influenced by the religious and literary cultural inheritance at the time. Without doubt the views of ancient poets such as Homer and Hesiod helped form the world in which philosophers would emerge. Homer, for instance, speaks of the shade-like spectres of the deceased and the transience of life. Within the *Iliad* and *Odyssey*, many heroes are

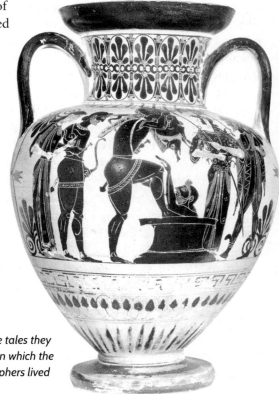

Poets like Homer and the tales they told shaped the world in which the classical philosophers lived

The work of Hippolytus of Rome provides much of our knowledge of Presocratic thought

considered paradigms of moral life, examples that later philosophers, such as Plato and Aristotle, referenced in their own works. Additionally, the tragedians, discussing complex issues of moral and civic life, were important contributors to the intellectual development and progress of the ancient Greek mind.

Religious life also, particularly in the Greek and Roman models, was not encumbered by the strictures of dogmatism. As a result, speculation and theory were allowed to develop. In addition, the myths, often transmitted by the epic poets and tragedians, are a type of pre-

Diogenes Laertius, who lived in the 3rd century AD, wrote one of the earliest histories of philosophy

philosophy. In his own history of philosophy in the first book of his *Metaphysics*, Aristotle says that the myth-lover is a philosopher, since myths are sources of wonder. Aristotle does not explain exactly how this is so, but a way to interpret this is that myths were often employed by his master Plato as symbolic of deeper philosophic truths. Myths were or could be metaphors or allegories for other truths, like the nature of the soul, the meaning of love and the human contemplation of mortality.

Much of classical philosophy persists to this day because of its transmission by, at times, hostile witnesses. The surviving work of the Presocratics is especially fragmentary, and their beliefs and sayings are quoted or paraphrased by multiple later authors. Well after the birth of Christ, Christians, keen to demonstrate the unorthodox paganism of the ancients, quoted the Presocratics and other later philosophers. Hippolytus in his *Refutation of All Heresies* is especially important as a witness to Presocratic thought, while Clement of Alexandria in *Stromata* explains the views of many ancient thinkers, philosophers among them. Ideological allies also preserved thoughts and opinions; for example, it was only the later Stoic authors who quoted the early Stoic teachers, absent in all other texts.

One author who garners perhaps too much criticism for his gossipy and eclectic collection of classical philosophy is Diogenes Laertius. Diogenes lived in the 3rd century AD and amassed a history of philosophy in ten books. Many of the facts and testimonies in his books appear nowhere else. However, for whatever reason, Diogenes does not always demonstrate a discriminating mind for philosophical nuance. Thus some scholars, glad that he has preserved much for us, see in him a rich resource, while others lament his work as insufficient and untrustworthy.

One interpretive difficulty is the degree of credulity we are to give to the texts. The quotations and personal history of some philosophers, we may gather, were selected for their headline appeal. Particularly outlandish quotations, taken out of context, were perhaps a choice tidbit for ancient ears. There is also the worry that antagonistic motives contributed to authors being portrayed in less than favourable lights. These worries are lessened, however, when multiple sources in the case of fragmentary authors, as well as holistic interpretive approaches, are applied to the philosophers.

In conclusion, to obtain the broadest possible view of classical philosophy, both the progression and breadth of thought should be kept in mind. Some authors may appeal more than others, just as some may be clearer and more understandable. To achieve a sense of what classical philosophy is made up of, this book is a good beginning.

Chapter 2

Thales, Anaximander, Anaximenes

Thales (6th century BC) is canonically the first philosopher in ancient Greece. He, along with two other philosophers from Miletus in modern day Turkey, Anaximenes and Anaximander, are considered Milesian Presocratics, this second term simply denoting that they were philosophically active before Socrates. Miletus was a city on the borders of Greek civilization at the time of Thales, in the 6th century BC. We arrive at this date because of an eclipse, dated 585BC, which he predicted. The prediction of the eclipse was promised to unfold within one year, and as it happened, came about dramatically during a battle between Medes and Lydians.

■ PRINCIPLES OF THE EARLY PRESOCRATICS	
Philosopher	**Principle (*arche*) of Universe**
Thales	Water
Anaximander	The Indefinite/Boundless
Anaximenes	Air

Remarkable Sage

Given Thales' prediction of an eclipse, he was perhaps less purely theoretical than the stereotype of an ancient philosopher might suggest. In fact, he was more like a sage or an all-around intellectual, as we shall

Thales is traditionally described as the first of the Greek philosophers

see in several anecdotes that have survived from antiquity. The most famous story of Thales concerns his astronomical preoccupations. Plato related the story of a female slave who reproached Thales because, while gazing upwards, he fell into a well. The absent-minded philosopher was eager to discover the secrets of heaven, but unaware of what was beneath his feet or behind him, the female slave chided. The Greek word for 'behind', *opisthen*, can also mean 'future', implying that while Thales could predict the nebulous future of the heavens, he could not see what was plainly on the ground behind him. Even today, philosophers are often accused of being focused only on their own abstract concerns and inept when it comes to practical matters.

Thales was chided by his slave for his focus on otherworldly matters, and once he even fell into a well because he was watching the sky rather than where he was going

Thales, reacting to these criticisms, decided to use his knowledge of the sky to predict that there would soon be a bumper crop of ripe olives. He shrewdly bought out all the olive presses in anticipation of this bounty. When the time came, his olive press monopoly allowed him to leverage significant profit.

Creative thinkers were often enlisted in matters of war.

Thales bought all the olive presses to make a healthy profit from his knowledge of the seasons

Herodotus, a Greek historian, described how Thales directed Croesus' army to dig a large trench, effectively rerouting the river behind the army, which allowed them to cross the Halys River. In another story, Thales demonstrated his knowledge of geometry, which he was said to have first introduced to the Greeks, in estimating the height of the Egyptian pyramids. The simple, yet ingenious method involved observing the hour of the day when his own shadow was the same length as his actual height, then measuring the pyramid's shadow at the same time of day. By this method, he accurately gauged it to be of parallel height without the difficulty of scaling the steep peak.

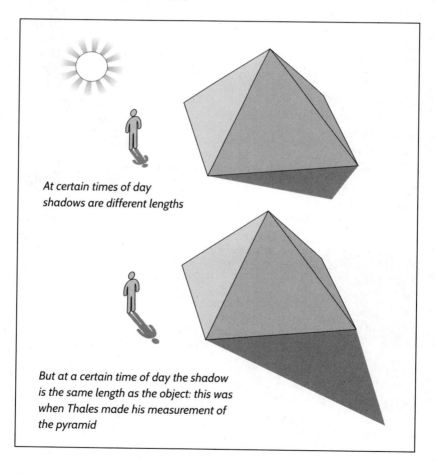

At certain times of day shadows are different lengths

But at a certain time of day the shadow is the same length as the object: this was when Thales made his measurement of the pyramid

The First Philosopher of Natural Explanation

If we return to Thales as a philosopher, we note that he was the first thinker who eschewed mythological explanations for the physical world. In fact, our word 'physics' derives from the Greek word *physis*, meaning nature, and it was as one of the first *physikoi* or inquirers in nature that Thales gained his philosophical reputation. As we will see, the Presocratic philosophers attempted to explain the world by appeals to *arche* (or plural *archai*). An *arche* is hard to interpret, because it was a term used by ancient philosophers to describe what each one thought was the best candidate to explain the way the world was. As we look into more Presocratics with their own *archai*, this term will become clearer. For now, it is best to consider an *arche* to be an explanatory principle or elemental cause of why the world is the way it is.

Water as the Principle of Explanation

Thales' *arche* was water. At first, water, as some kind of explanation for the universe, seems odd. Yet when we consider it more closely, as in the case for many *archai*, water does have several suitable features as to why it might be the fundamental principle of the world. Aristotle conjectures that Thales favoured water because living things seem to come from moist things, since

even seeds, their ultimate genesis, are themselves moist. Furthermore, we could add that the ready metamorphosis of water into ice and steam, and seemingly endless cycles of this phenomenon, might suggest an unusual dynamism and plasticity to water. If we take into

Thales believed that the earth floated on a vast sea – but he never explained what that sea rested on

account our dependence on water, we might think it alone is what life truly depends on. The ubiquity of water and its ability to sustain biological life may have prompted Thales to say that even lifeless things have souls, pronouncing that 'all things are full of gods'. Thales also believed that the earth floats on water; a conjecture that Aristotle reproved for not offering an explanation of what the water rested on.

ANAXIMANDER

Anaximander (c.610–546BC) was a student of Thales and also lived in Miletus. The Suidas, an ancient compendium of biographical data about Greek notables, tells us that he wrote *On Nature*, *The Period of the Earth*, *On the Stars*, *The Sphere*, and other works. These early Presocratic philosophers were concerned with both the astronomical or meteorological and what would come to be more clearly defined as philosophical interests.

The Indefinite

Like Thales before him, Anaximander was also a *physikos*, an inquirer into nature, and he offered his own *arche* to explain the nature of things. Anaximander's *arche*, unlike the very palpable water of Thales, was the *apeiron*. This Greek word can be translated as the Indefinite, the Infinite or the Boundless.

Anaximander's crucial contribution to philosophy was the idea of the 'Indefinite', which he used as his own arche to explain the nature of things

In asserting the Indefinite as the material cause, Anaximander was consciously rivalling Thales' preference for water, as well as any other candidates that might serve as a causal explanation for the world. Of course, the indefiniteness of the Indefinite has led commentators to different opinions on the nature of the Indefinite. One reading is that the *apeiron* is meant to exclude a sense of spatial boundedness, while another train of thought is that Anaximander's focus was on an ability to generate all things that are. Here, the idea is that while the Indefinite is no one thing strictly by nature, it can assume or produce in some manner the nature of many, if not all, things. Later authors quoting Anaximander's pronouncements about the Indefinite have added that it is ageless and eternal.

Aristotle tells us that Anaximander believed that the Indefinite was distinct from earth, air, fire and water, the four elements that many ancient philosophers incorporated in their explanations of the world order. This is important, as Aristotle explains that, for example, air is cold and fire is hot. Because they are opposites and cancel each other, the Indefinite could not be water, for if that were the case then fire would never come about, since water would prevent it by quenching. For this reason, Aristotle interprets the Indefinite as something in between two opposites such as fire and water. As an intermediate thing, it avoids the difficulty of how one element might come about in the presence of its opposite.

Opposites

As things are created in the world, opposites are separated out from the Indefinite. This use of the concept of opposites first appears in Anaximander and will later be deployed, with different interpretations, by other Presocratics. In Anaximander, it is clothed in the poetic language of justice and injustice. This language is meant to get across the idea that, when we have in mind two opposites, such as heat and cold, cold comes to be at the expense of heat. That is, the hot no longer exists when there is cold. Yet when the circumstances arise for there to be cold, there is reciprocity, a 'justice' that comes about as the cold in turn replaces the heat.

ANAXIMENES

Anaximenes (*c*.585–528BC) was a pupil of Anaximander, as Anaximander was of Thales. His *arche* was air, and, along with Thales and Anaximander, he created the foundations for the rich tradition of Presocratic philosophy.

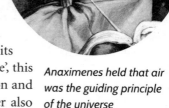

The World

Just as Thales before him, Anaximander also speculated on the cosmology of the world. He said that a fiery sphere surrounded the earth after its creation and that, like 'bark around a tree', this fire was broken off to form the sun, moon and stars. As this idea suggests, Anaximander also affirmed that the earth was a kind of cylinder. In fact, he used the image of a Greek column to describe the shape of the earth, noting that humans live on the flat top of the column of the earth.

Anaximenes held that air was the guiding principle of the universe

In direct contrast to Thales, Anaximander claimed that the earth does not depend on any substance, such as water, for its stability. Rather the

Fiery sphere

Earth

The sun, moon and stars are excess from the fiery sphere

earth maintains its position by equilibrium, an explanation that seems to depend on both balance and necessity. However, perhaps inspired by Thales' conjectures about water, Anaximander posited that the first animals came forth from moisture, presumably meaning large bodies of water. He speculated that mankind arose when a fish-like creature gestated humans and gave birth to them.

Anaximenes, in the tradition of these predecessors, posited that air was the *arche* from which things came into being. It is not surprising that multiple ancient authors record that Anaximenes attributed divinity to air. For although not a conventional god, air, like Thales' water and Anaximander's the Indefinite, fulfilled a role of creation and governance previously occupied by appeals to mythology and religion. Anaximenes believed that the soul was merely air, as the Greek word *pneuma* implies both breath and air. Just as our soul, as a certain kind of air, is a principle of order in our bodies, so the air in the world orders and controls the world at large.

In Anaximenes' conception, air, through a process, changes in its essence into other things. What begins as air can change to fire by becoming thinner or rarefied. Likewise, by becoming thicker it can, in turn, change to wind, cloud, air, and earth, while last and most dense of all it can become stone. Also like Anaximander, Anaximenes incorporated the idea of the Indefinite, but he used it in his description of air, claiming that it was in some sense unlimited. All things, he claimed, could come from air by becoming either more dense and therefore more cold, or more rarefied and therefore more hot. With this explanation, Anaximenes not only could explain how apparently different things, such as clouds and rocks, could arise, but other qualitative differences as well. Thus all differences could be related in terms of similarity: everything was really air of one sort or another.

Air as the explanation of other matter

THINNER   THICKER

FIRE ← **AIR** → WIND → CLOUD → AIR → EARTH → STONE

The most obvious examples of this phenomenon are fire and ice, respectively, but there is also the ingenuous proof used by Anaximenes for breath. He said that when we blow through pursed lips the air feels cool because it is condensed, while when we open our mouth wide and exhale, our breath is hot because it has been rarefied.

Anaximenes, in the Milesian habit, also pronounced upon the state of the heavens. Heavenly bodies, the earth itself, as well as the sun and the moon are all flat and, in Anaximenes' metaphor, ride upon the air the way a lid covers an opening. Anaximenes is able to give an account of diverse natural phenomena like meteorology and geology by appealing to air. Clouds form when air condenses, which in turn can lead to a cascading process of condensation that first results in rain, then snow and, finally, the relatively dense material of hail. Earthquakes occur because of the excess or deficiency of water leading either to saturated weakness or arid cracking in the soil of the earth, respectively. The intrinsic satisfaction and curiosity of seeking explanations, as shown by Greek philosophers in general, is evidenced by the fact that they even sought to explain the world around them in its entirety. Anaximenes, for example, described the rainbow quite mundanely as the resistance of a dense cloud to the rays of the sun.

Key points

- Living in the 6th century BC, Thales is considered to be the first philosopher because he shifted explanations from the theological or mythological to the natural and gained his philosophical reputation as one of the first *physikoi*, or inquirers after nature.

- Thales proposed that the *arche*, or explanatory principle for the world, was water because of its pervasiveness, ability to sustain biological life, and apparent dynamism and plasticity.

- Anaximander's explanatory principle for the world was the *apeiron*, the Infinite, from which opposites, such as the cold and hot, derive, and due to the apparent cyclical nature of their appearance, are described as realizing justice and injustice.

- Anaximenes proposed that the earth, shaped like a column, maintained its position by equilibrium, and that the excess matter from a fiery sphere surrounding it gave rise to other heavenly bodies.

- Anaximenes believed that the soul was a type of air and given the soul's unique governing properties, applied this same dynamism to the air, proposing it was the explanatory material principle which, when dense or when rarefied, gave rise to other elements such as water, fire and ice.

Chapter 3

Anaxagoras

THE MIND

Anaxagoras (c.510–428BC) was renowned as a learned man in antiquity and reported as being the teacher of Pericles, the famous statesman; Thucydides, the great historian; and he even instructed Socrates. Anaxagoras was also described as the disciple of Anaximenes. He garnered the somewhat contemptuous nickname 'Mind' because of the important role the mind came to play in his philosophy. Of the several accounts of his death, one says he was put on trial in absentia at age 70 for his belief that the sun was molten metal, an opinion which brought into doubt the divinity of the sun. Preferring death to imprisonment, he reportedly said that nature condemned him to death long ago. A number of anecdotes demonstrate his indifference to the grave. When confronted with the unexpected death of his son he said, 'I knew I begat a mortal', a sentiment which reputedly ended up in a play of the Greek tragedian Euripides. He quipped that there are two rehearsals

Anaxagoras taught many of the great figures in Greek history, including Pericles, Thucydides and Socrates

Anaxagoras was notoriously indifferent to death, a sentiment that made its way into one of Euripides' plays

for death, the time before birth and the time before sleep. On his deathbed, asked if he wished to return to his home town of Clazomenae, he said it was unnecessary, because all the paths to the underworld are the same. It was perhaps in light of such pessimism that he was inevitably asked why someone would prefer to live rather than not be born. His response was 'to observe the sky and order of the universe'. For Anaxagoras, the goal of life was observation and from this arose freedom.

The Universe's Composition

Anaxagoras had a somewhat unusual account of the nature of the universe. He conceptualized things as belonging to either that which is homogeneous, or all of the same kind; and that which is not homogeneous, or which is mixed together. The homogeneous 'stuff', as we may call it, never came to be nor will it ever be destroyed, it just is. Anaxagoras believed at the beginning of the universe that everything was mixed together. He called this physical stuff unlimited or infinite. Later, there was a great separation, wherein things came to be called by their different names.

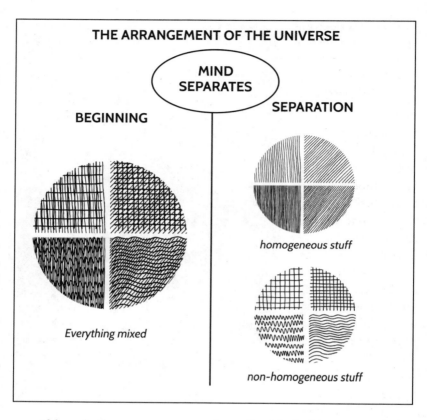

THE ARRANGEMENT OF THE UNIVERSE

MIND SEPARATES

BEGINNING

SEPARATION

homogeneous stuff

Everything mixed

non-homogeneous stuff

Although there was a separation of a kind, things nevertheless remained mixed. In the mixture of each thing, whatever came to predominate gave the object its name. A contemporary example of this is gold, which is characterized by the level of purity for cosmetic jewellery. Among other categories, there is 14K gold, 18K gold, and 24K gold – each of them is called gold.

■ NAMES ARE GIVEN BY WHATEVER PREDOMINATES	
Gold	
14K	**More gold**
18K	The purest gold is not 100% gold though
24K	

Life's Salad

In fact, we do not even care whether the impure content mixed in with the gold is iron or is sediment. We still call it gold. There is another interpretation of Anaxagoras' conception of things being mixed together. The conventional understanding is that there is a mixing of the homogeneous with the non-homogeneous, such as in the gold example opposite. But there is also the possibility that he's proposing that things in the universe are inextricably bound up with each other, much like the way parts of a salad together constitute a salad.

Returning to the conventional reading, a later commentator made the point that Anaxagoras may have formulated his theory for two reasons. The first owes to the idea that nothing comes from nothing. There has to be something to begin with, from which a subsequent, second thing becomes. So insistent was Anaxagoras on this idea that he said that coming to be is nothing more than being mixed together, and perishing was nothing more than the dissolution of that mixture. The second reason was arrived at by example, such as in the case of human

Gold is called 'gold' regardless of its purity

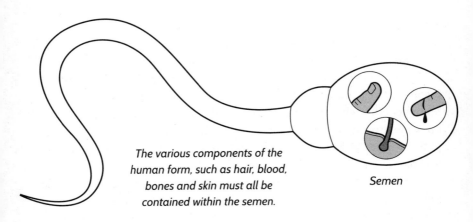

The various components of the human form, such as hair, blood, bones and skin must all be contained within the semen.

Semen

semen. There must be bits of hair, nail, bone, skin, blood and so forth latent within the semen, which in turn gives rise to the eventual baby. For how else, he must have reasoned, could a human form arise from something so different as semen?

Anaxagoras concluded that there always remains more of any stuff inside of the secondary stuff. He observed that things arise out of all kinds of other things: trees come from dirt, humans from semen, flies (apparently) from corpses, and so forth. Adhering to the belief that nothing can come from nothing, he postulated that within each type of stuff, there must be mixed in an unlimited supply of other stuff. That is, within the flesh, there is cheese, and within the cheese, more stones, and within the stones, water, and so on and so forth, ad infinitum.

Lucretius, a later Roman philosopher (see chapter 17), sought to show the absurdity of this doctrine by imagining that when we crush corn under the mill, if Anaxagoras were correct, we should expect to see a bit of blood or anything other than corn present itself. Yet we only see corn. Anaxagoras' point, more literally, was that there is always a smaller, never a smallest, and never a larger, but always a largest. One interpreter has claimed that this is meant to establish the upper and lower limit for the ingredients of a mixture. For simplicity's sake, imagine a ball of clay, into which you place some pea-sized gravel. You can always add more clay, in the process making the clay larger but never the largest, and by taking away some of the original gravel you put in, you can make the

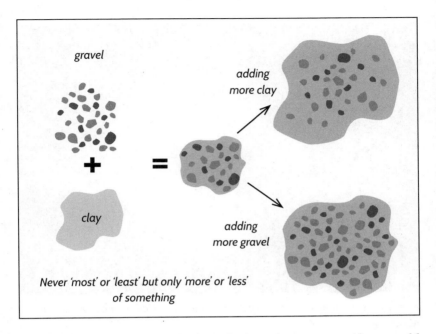

gravel

adding
more clay

+

=

clay

adding
more gravel

*Never 'most' or 'least' but only 'more' or 'less'
of something*

gravel lesser, but you can never have the least, because even if you could take out the gravel (something Anaxagoras would not concede), this would not be the least gravel but none at all.

The Role of Mind

Another of Anaxagoras' principles, equally important as the material stuff of which the universe is composed, was a self-ruling and independent principle called Mind. Mind or Intellect (Greek *Nous*) was the ruler and as such ordered and separated everything off in the beginning. Mind brought this about by a literal revolution, and it is by means of this revolving that things continue to be separated off from each other. This Mind, moreover, is the cause of motion in all things, while none of the things that exist influences Mind in any way. The motion caused by Mind is nothing other than the separation mentioned above. It was perhaps the observable rotation of the heavens at night that inspired Anaxagoras to come up with the idea of a separation resulting from a revolution. It should be understood that Mind is completely independent from the physical makeup of the universe, yet it causes the universe to be the way

Anaxagoras' explanation of an eclipse was remarkably close to modern scientific reasoning

that it is. Anaxagoras' theory of Mind garnered as much criticism as did his physical theory. Both Plato and Aristotle criticized him on this point; Aristotle laying down the charge that Anaxagoras lazily trotted out the concept of Mind as a kind of *deus ex machina*.

Anaxagoras applied his theory to a physical explanation of things. For example, he said that the rainbow was a reflection of the sun in the clouds. By understanding that the rainbow, as a reflection, was a kind of mixture of sun and cloud, he was able to give an account of the phenomenon within the context of his own philosophical system. Along with his predecessors, he gave naturalistic explanations of geological and cosmological phenomena. The flat earth rides on air and earthquakes are the result of a turbulence of this air under the earth. He also made theoretical attempts at explanations, which sound familiar to us today, such as eclipses are the interposition of one celestial body between the earth and a second body, the heat from the sun and others stars is not felt because of their distance from us, and the moon is much closer to us than the sun.

Key points

- Anaxagoras' basic explanations of the universe can be boiled down to two principles, physical stuff and Mind.

- Anaxagoras proposed that at the beginning everything was mixed together and that this physical stuff was unlimited. There was always more stuff inside other stuff, no matter how much was taken out.

- After the great separation of stuff, things nevertheless remained mixed and whatever stuff came to predominate came to be called by that name.

- Mind was and is separate from the physical stuff of the universe; the stuff does not affect it at all, but on the other hand, Mind absolutely controls it by arranging it and causing the motion of separation of all things.

- Anaxagoras gave naturalistic explanations of celestial phenomena, including eclipses, heat from the sun and stars, and distances from planets, often strikingly prescient to our modern scientific explanations.

Chapter 4

Empedocles

EMPEDOCLES: NATURE AND THE COSMOS

Empedocles (c.490–430BC) was born, it is believed, shortly after Anaxagoras. In a philosophical line that stretches before and after him, he wrote on nature and the cosmos, in addition to medicine. Although a foreign notion in contemporary philosophy, Empedocles, like other ancient philosophers, composed his philosophy in poetic meter. The fragments that have survived of his poems are from two works, *On Nature* and *Cleansings*. In the few remaining fragments from the end of his poem *On Nature*, Empedocles seems to acknowledge a type of god, who is contrasted with mortal creatures, whom Empedocles believed to be nothing more than the accumulation

Empedocles wrote extensively on nature and the cosmos

of random biological parts. This god was without human features nor does he have branches like plant life, nor any biological mode of propagation such as genitals or seed, but he is said to dart around the universe with his swift thoughts. This description is similar to that of the cosmos as a sphere, which was also described as without branches, limbs or genitals, but it is unclear if this god is to be identified as the cosmos, or what relation, if any, they have.

The Four 'Roots' or Elements of Things

Empedocles believed in the reliability of the senses, in so far as they go, but was realistic about the limits and depths of their knowledge. Empedocles was the first to propose four elements, which he called 'Roots': Shining Zeus, Life-bearing Hera, Aidoneus and Nestis. Whether these were meant literally or as a poetic appropriation of mythology, they were stand-ins for fire, air, earth and water.

■ EMPEDOCLES' ELEMENTS		
Four Roots	**Elements**	**Symbol**
Zeus	Fire	▲
Hera	Air	■
Aidoneus	Earth	●
Nestis	Water	≈

It is these more prosaic characterizations that later philosophers utilize. Empedocles believed that at the beginning, air was first separated, then fire, earth, and finally water.

Cosmic Cycle of the Universe

In what has been termed a Cosmic Cycle, Empedocles said that these four Roots are brought together and separated by forces he calls, respectively, Love and Strife.

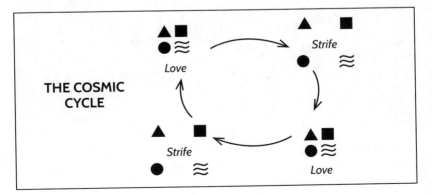

Love, as one might expect, brings Roots together, while Strife forces them apart. There is a timeless continuity to this cycle, because, while all things transition from the four Roots, changed by the unification of Love or the dissolution of Strife, the Cosmic Cycle, in this state of perpetual cycling, remains the same. The stasis of the cosmos illuminates Empedocles' commitment to the idea that nothing comes to be or passes away. Nothing new is added to the cosmos or taken away, rather earth, air, water and fire each takes its turn, as it is brought about by Love or Strife.

A consequence of this view is that Empedocles commits to saying that, despite appearances to the contrary, there are no births or deaths. In Empedocles' scheme, what seems to be the creation or death of a new

A painting may be composed of subjects like people and even paint itself is composed of different colours mixed together – just like the 'Roots' that combine and intertwine to form the universe

human is merely the momentary cosmic shift toward a grouping of Roots which results, by Love, into their forming a man, or by Strife, into the same man's death. Thus, when someone is said to be created, in fact he already existed in the form of Roots, and when he dies, he continues to exist in the form of Roots. Empedocles depicts the Cosmic Cycle in one passage as a chase, wherein Love pursues Strife, and in the process countless mixtures of animals and plants spring forth.

A striking metaphor about the Cosmic Cycle, devised by Empedocles, was of a painting. We see people and animals in a painting. In fact, though, they are merely paint, corresponding by analogy to the way reality is composed of Roots. Likewise, the paint is itself often a mixture of two or more colours, such as yellow and blue for green, illustrating the idea that mixtures of the Roots combine to create the things of our universe.

Zoology and Biology

Empedocles also gave speculative consideration to zoological matters. One ancient commentator, Aetius, preserves four successive stages in which animals and plants came to be. First, living things consisted only

■ FOUR STAGES OF BIOLOGICAL GENERATION

1. Disjointed limbs

2. Monsters with mismatched limbs

3. Whole animals

4. Whole animals by sexual reproduction

of disjointed limbs here and there. Aristotle quotes Empedocles saying that there were faces without necks and eyes without faces. Second, due to the happenstance arrangement of these limbs, fabulous monsters came about. Third, there came about what he termed animals with a whole nature. Fourth and lastly, there is a stage in which animals came about not as a result of a mixture of the four elements, but by some cause which effected them either internally, such as the digestion of food, or externally, such as the 'mixing' which occurs between animals when they mate and breed.

In the midst of criticism of this biology, Aristotle depicts Empedocles' theory as one which very much sounds like a prototype of natural selection as Darwin envisioned it thousands of years later. Those creatures which were suitably and fortunately compounded of the right parts survived, while those which had unsuitable unions of various parts did not. According to Empedocles, there were creatures with two faces on either side of the head, hermaphrodites unable to breed, and oxen with the faces of men.

Elsewhere Empedocles notes that hair, leaves, feathers and scales are the same type of thing. Empedocles' observation is an objection to the idea that the parts of a body have in some way been deliberately arranged. That is, the parts which we call feathers could just as easily have come about on humans, and the parts which we call hair could plausibly have arisen on the skin of birds. The way of life for humans and birds would undoubtedly have changed in such a scenario, but hair and feathers are similar enough as parts that they could be interchanged, with only a change of function. In fact, we might have expected both birds and humans to have hair, or both of them to have feathers. Because of the different, though structurally similar, features that arise on different animals, Empedocles emphasized the role of chance in the body parts of animals.

Reincarnation

Despite the appearance that Empedocles' philosophy leaned heavily on random chance, his doctrine of reincarnation highlights the role that Love and Strife played in his cosmology and biology. If someone were to commit murder, he must spend 30,000 years being cyclically

Empedocles claimed that he had previously lived lives as a boy, a girl, a bush, a bird, and a fish

reincarnated into the difficult lives of a variety of mortal creatures. Empedocles says that this act is to have put one's trust in Strife, who is mad. It must be inferred from this that he must mean that a murder creates separation of another human from the rest of creation, or from each of his body parts from themselves, as the corpse decays. It also shows that mankind is not at the mercy of chance, for we have the opportunity to follow Love and not Strife, at least in the limited scenario of choosing to murder or not.

Of course, with reincarnation, murder can also be broadened beyond the human sphere. Empedocles bemoans the fact that he was not destroyed before the first time he had eaten flesh. In an admission of his own reincarnation, he said that he was previously boy, girl, bush, bird and fish. In a striking picture, drawing on his personal suspicions of guilt, he imagines a father about to slay a sacrificial animal, ignorant of the fact that he is going to kill his reincarnated son or father, obstinate to the reality that the terrible sounds of the animal's fears are really the screams of his own kin.

Sight and Perception

Empedocles had a theory of sight, which he apparently extended to all the senses, which has been related to us by Plato and others. He believed that from each thing that is, there is an emanation or outflow. In the appropriate sense organ, there are holes that, if appropriately sized and shaped, can receive these emanations. As a result, we can only perceive sound through the ears and some things are too bright to see or too small

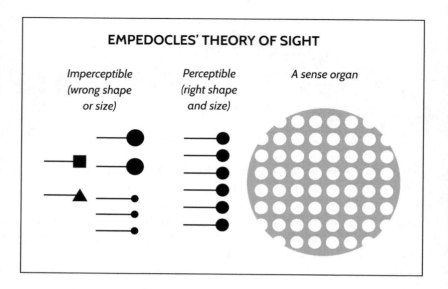

to touch such as air, because the emanations coming off them do not fit into the perceptual holes in our body.

One can immediately see the affinity of this perceptual theory with his theory of biological generation. Both depend on chance for a successful outcome, suitably fitted limbs for an animal and suitably fitted emanations for perception. This theory of perception depends, at a more abstract level, on the idea of 'like by like', which Empedocles applied to thoughts as well. What this means is not only that the perceiving hole in each sense organ must be like the emanation it is perceiving, but also that there must be a source of light (fire) in the eye for it to perceive light colours and some source of sound in the ear for it to perceive sound. The theory gets even more specific than this, for Empedocles states flatly that 'with earth do we see earth, with water water, with air shining air, and destructive fire with fire'. He may have had in mind nothing other than the fact that we are composed, like everything is, out of those four elements, or he may have been implying something subtler and more complex. In the arena of thought, Empedocles advocated for the idea that it too proceeded by like by like. When speaking about thought, he must have intended something like understanding or comprehension, for he also maintained that ignorance proceeds by unlike by unlike.

Key points

- Empedocles was the first philosopher to propose the four elements of fire, air, earth, and water, which he called 'Roots', referring to them as the Greek gods Zeus, Hera, Aidoneus and Nestis.

- In Empedocles' Cosmic Cycle, the four Roots were brought together and separated, respectively, by Love and Strife.

- As a result of both the persistence of the four Roots and the turn-taking cycle of Love and Strife, Empedocles was committed to the idea that nothing really comes into or out of existence.

- Empedocles held to a crude form of natural selection, wherein mortal creatures such as animals are nothing more than the accumulation of body parts, initially found scattered about, but not forming a complete animal; eventually those collections of body parts that survived became what we term animals.

- Empedocles' theory of perception depended on the idea that emanations came from perceptible objects and entered into appropriately receptive holes in our sense organs, which, based on like by like, must be like the emanation it is perceiving.

Chapter 5

Parmenides and Zeno

PARMENIDES: METAPHYSICAL MONISM

Parmenides (c.515–mid-5th century BC) was a philosopher and poet, adapting the medium of poetry like other Greek philosophers such as Empedocles, composing a single work of which large sections have been preserved. Like the work of many ancient Greek philosophers, this work was titled *On Nature*. Yet his was not a philosophy for the common crowd; even in antiquity, both the coarseness of his style and the obscurity of his philosophy garnered criticism and stoked interest. Parmenides' outlook has sometimes been termed 'metaphysical monism'. What this means, simply, is that he thought the fundamental nature of reality was one and unified. As a consequence, this makes it easier to understand his criticism of those who both think and say what is not. Those who say that there are many things, asserting that they come into being and pass away, are thinking and speaking

Parmenides' philosophy was obscure and coarsely written, but attracted the discussion of many ancient Greek philosophers

falsehood and opinion. This may include humans themselves or even the fundamental principles posited by previous philosophers, such as fire, air or mind. There is only that which is the universe.

The Proem of *On Nature*

The first long fragment we have of *On Nature* is commonly referred to as the 'proem'. This preface sets the metaphorical and dramatic tone for the message which Parmenides is set to deliver. It begins with the majestic opening line, 'The horses carry me and they ably convey me according to the wish of my heart, when they set out to lead me on the world-renowned way of the demi-god, which carries the man who knows across all cities'. As Parmenides continues on, the setup is ever more fabulous with the daughters of the sun leading the way, the horses being very wise, and Parmenides himself being transported in a chariot. Parmenides is brought to the gates of the roads of night and day. These gates are locked and watched over by personified Justice.

PARMENIDES' GATES OF ROADS OF NIGHT AND DAY

This goddess, Justice, greets him and allays the fears he has for the long distance he has strayed from the land of mortals. She tells him that he will inquire of all things, both the 'steadfast heart of well-rounded truth' and the 'opinions of mortals'. The revelatory mode of this dramatic presentation emphasizes the importance of the claims that Parmenides is going to declare. The truths, in fact, are nothing less than the realities and appearances of the universe.

Truth or Opinion

The goddess asks Parmenides, after their brief introduction, to pick one of two paths. He can pick only one of the paths and will be obligated to carry this account with him. The paths, already difficult enough in the midst of elaborate, symbolic poetry, become even more abstruse. The first path corresponds to the truth: 'it is and it is impossible for it not to be'. The second is false: 'IT is not and it is necessary for IT not to be'. These paths are described as the way of truth and the way of opinion.

In a further explanation of the second way of opinion, the goddess warns Parmenides not to give in to the conventional way of thinking, to join in the common opinion by conceding that, 'things which are not are'. This confusing statement has been construed in the following two ways, which depend on the meaning of 'are'. The first is to understand it to mean that things that do not exist cannot be said to exist. On this reading, it is simply nonsense, a flat-out contradiction, for something that does not exist to exist. An alternative is to interpret the phrase 'things which are not are' to mean that 'things which are not are not things because nothing can be said about them'. That is, in this second option, we cannot say of 'nothing' that it is brown, or heavy, or tasty, or affix any determinate quality or description to it; one simply cannot speak of nothing in this manner.

■ TWO MEANINGS OF 'IS'		
Subject	'IS'	Example
X	exists	Socrates exists
X	is Y	Socrates is mortal

Two-Headed Mankind

Whichever of these two alternatives Parmenides has in mind, there is also a close association between the meaning of 'is' that he is arguing for and the ability to think or speak about this 'is'. He says that to take the way of opinion, to consider that 'which is not is', is both to think and to say something which is impossible. Evidently, what Parmenides is trying to get across is the idea that to think or to speak is to think or speak of *something*. It makes no sense to claim you are referring to something when it does not exist, and nothing can be said of something that does

Mankind is 'two-headed', constantly being torn between two alternative paths and unsure which to take

not exist. To claim that nothing exists is to manifestly speak (or think) a contradiction: the very meaning of nothing is that it is nothing, it cannot be thought or spoken of. To bring this back one step, Parmenides could say that not only can you not speak or think of what is not, but also you cannot even learn of this nothingness, for it does not exist. In the context of this discussion of the two ways, Parmenides or rather the goddess speaking on his behalf, depicts mankind as being 'two-headed', unable to decide on which path to take or perhaps inconsistently taking both. He chastises people for trusting experience, whereas they should trust in the validity of his 'contentious refutation'.

Reality is One

As Parmenides continues, he hones in on the nature of the right way, that which we can say actually is, which is nothing other than reality, the universe itself. He tells us that the signs or indications along this path reveal that reality is uncreated, indestructible, whole, unique, unshakeable and complete. It is uncreated and indestructible, he argues, because for it to come into being would have meant that it had to be nothing first. But this is impossible, as he argued earlier. Likewise, it cannot be destroyed, for this would show that reality is not being or does not possess existence. For to exist is to exist, and to be destroyed is to not exist. The strictures of this kind of argumentation of the nature of reality lead Parmenides to poetically claim that necessity holds the universe in the bonds of limit, hemmed in equally on all sides, comparing it to a perfect sphere.

ZENO

Zeno (c.490–430BC) was the disciple of Parmenides. There is a Platonic dialogue named the *Parmenides*, in which Parmenides and Zeno, nearly 25 years younger, visit a young Socrates. From this and other sources Zeno is represented as defending the notion, explicated above, that the nature of reality is one. Zeno's method was a vigorous defence of his master Parmenides and an attempt to turn the tables on those who claimed reality was many instead of one. In their attacks, foes of Parmenides lodged objections that showed if we were to assume reality is one, many absurdities logically follow. In defiance, Zeno's work was an explicit attempt to show the absurdities of the view that reality is many.

Zeno of Elea was a passionate defender of his master, Parmenides

Many of these proofs have come down to us in the form of paradoxes (for it is assumed that they must be false), but it is often difficult to penetrate and pinpoint the exact error of Zeno.

Achilles and the Tortoise

Aristotle recorded several of these paradoxes, the most famous of which is sometimes called Achilles and the Tortoise, although no tortoise is mentioned. In this scenario, imagine a slower runner with a head start over a faster runner. The faster runner, claims Zeno, can never overtake the slower runner. The reason is that the faster runner always only reaches the point where the slower runner had already begun, but that subsequently the slower runner is at a new point, at which place the faster runner must now catch up to him, and so the chase continues forevermore. The faster runner, having to reach an infinite series of these points, never overtakes the slower runner. Since this is so, there is no motion, and without motion reality cannot be said to be many.

The Runner in the Stadium

Similar to this example is that of the runner in the stadium. In this example, we imagine a runner aiming to quickly reach the finish line of the race. But before he gets to the finish line, he must first make his way to the halfway point of the racetrack. But before he gets to the halfway point, he must first make his way to the halfway point between the starting line and halfway point. This halving of every target means that our poor runner will never reach his goal, because he always has a new halfway point to reach his mark.

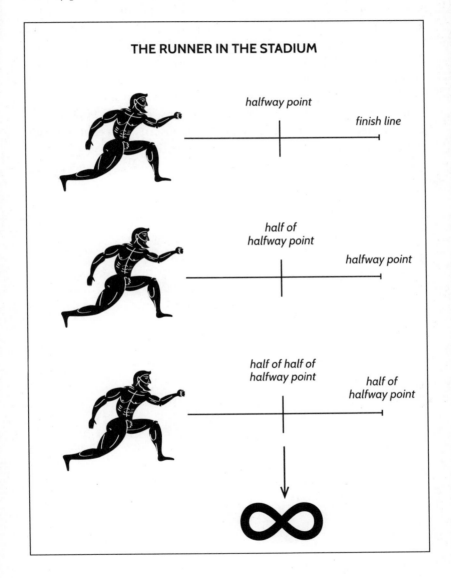

THE RUNNER IN THE STADIUM

halfway point

finish line

half of halfway point

halfway point

half of half of halfway point

half of halfway point

∞

Besides rejecting motion, Zeno also appealed to the absurdity of the notion of plurality itself. In this argument, he described a situation in which reality, if it is plural, is both finite and infinite. It is finite because, if the plurality is just as much as it is, and no more, then it is finite and limited. More complicatedly, he argued that plurality is infinite. His argument proceeded like this: Take objects A and B. For them to be considered two separate things, there must be a third object C, which distinguishes them. Now we have three objects, A, B and C, and yet, for example, A and C must be distinguished by appeal to a fourth object, D. This process can never cease, and so in this way reality, as plurality, is infinite. Thus, combining both conclusions, reality is both a finite plurality and an infinite plurality, but this is absurd and a contradiction, therefore reality is not a plurality, but it is one.

Key points

- In Parmenides' philosophical poem there are two paths: the path of opinion and the path of truth, whereby he affirms that the state of the world exists as it is, and that to speak or to think about that which 'is not' is impossible, for something must first exist or be to speak of it or about it.

- Parmenides concludes that the universe must have always existed and will always exist, for this is what it means 'to be'; therefore, the universe is one and unchanging.

- Parmenides' disciple was Zeno, who was a zealous defender of his master's thesis of the unity of the universe.

- Zeno attempted to show that motion was impossible by a number of paradoxes of motion, including Achilles and the Tortoise, whereby Achilles can never catch up to the tortoise because he only ever reaches a point at which the tortoise was just at, and he must traverse an infinite number of such points.

- In the paradox of the Runner, a runner can never reach the finish line because he must first reach the halfway point of his goal, but he must first reach the halfway point of that, and then the halfway point of that, and so on, ad infinitum.

Chapter 6

Pythagoras and his Disciples

PYTHAGORAS: RELIGIOUS, MYSTICAL, PHILOSOPHICAL AND CULTIC

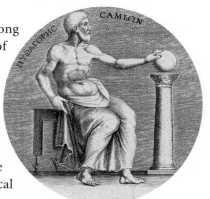

Pythagoras (*c.*570–495BC), along with his followers, is one of the most perplexing ancient philosophers. He was the head of a secretive sect and left behind no written work of his own. It is hard to pin down the figure of Pythagoras because he seems at once to have elements of the religious, mystical, philosophical and cultic. He was born on the island of Samos and left aged 40 to found a community in Croton in southern Italy in accordance with his beliefs.

Pythagoras is best known for the mathematical theorem bearing his name but his broad and insightful philosophy inspired a number of followers

Pythagoras was born on the island of Samos in Greece before leaving for Croton in southern Italy

It is reported that he influenced the people of that city to love frugality and virtue.

The most reliable and complete reports that we have of Pythagoras and Pythagoreanism are from Aristotle, yet they came hundreds of years after Pythagoras' lifetime. It is no wonder given the devotion of his acolytes and the secrecy of his school that Pythagoras was said to have a thigh of gold, to have provoked a river to speak to him, and claimed he was neither human nor divine. Within the philosophically charged atmosphere of ancient Greece, it is equally unsurprising that he had his share of detractors as well, including Heraclitus, who said he practised a fraudulent art.

Two Sects of Pythagoreans

Pythagorean, Aristotle tells us, is a term we can apply to the earliest group of the philosopher's disciples. They eagerly took up the study of mathematics, an interest that incidentally gave rise to the association of the Pythagorean theorem with its namesake. It should also be noted that music, with its close relationship to mathematics, was held in high regard as well, and it is said that through the serendipity of the musical chords Pythagoras first gained insight into the realities of numbers.

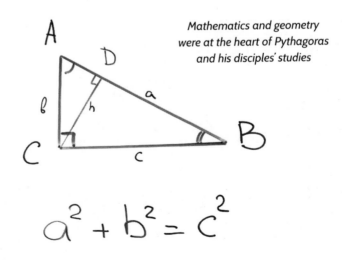

Mathematics and geometry were at the heart of Pythagoras and his disciples' studies

$$a^2 + b^2 = c^2$$

Music was one of many subjects held in high regard by Pythagoras and his disciples

Although Pythagoras reportedly held his disciples to a code of silence, presumably due to secrecy, it is not beyond reason that there was some musical rationale prompting this behaviour as well. A good representation of the peculiar mixture of geometry, music and mysticism was the Pythagorean tetractys. This symbol was a triangle formed from ten dots, starting with a row of one dot, then two dots, then three dots and then four dots. Within the dots countless other triangles can be connected and the four rows have the respective relations of 4:3, 3:2, and 2:1, corresponding to musical scales.

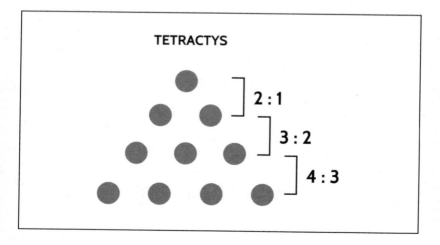

Reality in Numbers

Other philosophers such as Thales believed that water was the material principle of the universe (*arche*), while for Anaximenes air fulfilled this same role. The Pythagoreans believed that the principle of reality was number – a precursor to modern physics and its mathematical precision – yet, as plausible as this account may seem, the Pythagoreans did not limit their mathematical theory to tidy cosmic book-keeping. On the contrary, seeing resemblances of reality in numbers, they understood that, for example, justice and reason were simply a result of number. The things of reality, they proposed, exist as an imitation of number. So committed were they to the perfection of the numerical that, notwithstanding any observation to the contrary, these Pythagoreans decided to posit a tenth heavenly body, which they termed 'counter-earth', since only nine planets were deemed incomplete. They compressed and abstracted their mathematical theory down to the idea of the odd and even. The odd is limited while the even is unlimited, while the number one, because it is both even and odd, belongs to and proceeds from both, while number proceeds from the number one.

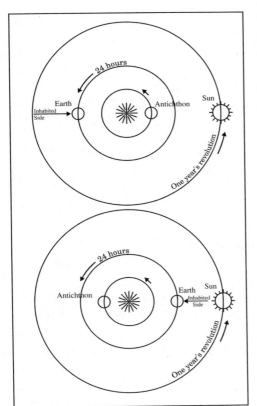

The Pythagoreans' belief in the principle of number meant they could not conceive of a cosmos with only nine heavenly bodies – and so they posited the idea of a 'counter-earth' or 'antichthon' to make an even ten

61

Table of Opposites

A second offshoot of Pythagorean philosophy, associated with Alcmaeon of Croton, has come to be called the Table of Opposites, also named by Aristotle. This list of opposites, ten pairs in all, starts with a similarity to the previous Pythagorean group. This group too have limited and unlimited, odd and even, but expand beyond this to include male and female, resting and moving, straight and curved, light and dark, good and bad, square and not square.

■ TABLE OF OPPOSITES	
Limited	**Unlimited**
Odd	Even
Unity	Plurality
Right	Left
Male	Female
Resting	Moving
Straight	Curved
Light	Darkness
Good	Evil
Square	Not square (oblong)

The first of each of these is considered to align or be coordinate to each other, just as the second of each pairing. For instance, male, resting and straight are in some relation, as are female, moving and curved. Much of the list is obscure and connections among the opposites difficult to determine. However, one remark preserved in Aristotle's work *Physics* gives us reason to appreciate the connection between three pairs of opposites: odd and even, limited and unlimited, and square and not square (uneven side lengths). In Aristotle's explanation, a series of dots or any shape is drawn into a grid pattern, around which successively bigger gnomons (imagine a carpenter's square) are placed. Depending on whether the first number inside the first gnomon is 1 or 2, then the subsequent gnomons will be, for 1, all 'odd' and have a 'square' shape. This series is 'limited' because this shape alone repeats. The grid starting with 2 will be 'even', as every one after will be also, and will result in each successive gnomon being of unequal length or 'not square'. The shape of every successive rectangle will have a different ratio of length to height and thus be 'unlimited'.

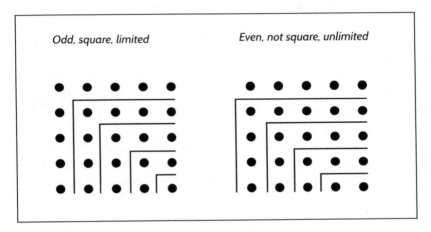

Odd, square, limited   *Even, not square, unlimited*

Oral Teachings

Several sources preserve Pythagoras' teachings, which he is said to have delivered orally. These teachings were divided into three parts: definitions of things, the superlatives and prohibitions.

Regarding prohibitions there appeared to be two kinds of teachings. The first were prohibitions which possessed, in an expectedly Pythagorean way, ceremonial and possibly ethical aspects. One of these was a prohibition on the eating of beans. Later writers in antiquity interpreted this rule in various ways: some declared that the prohibition owed to the beans' likeness to genitals, others claimed they resembled the gates of Hades, or were banned due to the destructiveness of the bean, their likeness to the nature of the universe, or because they were used to choose rulers by lot. Furthermore, others conjectured that beans caused flatulence and were thus undignified. Other injunctions of this kind included an order not to touch a white rooster, not to things that have fallen from the table, and not to touch sacred fish.

The second group of prohibitions were clever and short. These were not necessarily pithy aphorisms, but often had practical application hidden within a metaphorical shell. 'Do not poke the fire with a sword' was a warning not to annoy an angered man with sharp words. 'Do not eat the heart' was a reminder not to stew in your own despair. There was even advice for the end of life: 'When on a

The Pythagoreans issued a number of prohibitions, including a warning not to 'poke the fire with a sword', a metaphor instructing one not to insult angry men

trek, do not turn around' was a courageous call to not cling to life when close to death.

Symbola

The lists of superlatives were offered as an oral instruction, with short questions and even shorter answers: 'What is the most just thing? Sacrificing. What is the wisest thing? Number, but second is the person who assigned names. What is the most powerful thing? Knowledge. What is the best thing? Happiness.' Similarly, the oral teachings of definitions were offered as question and responses: 'What are the isles of the blessed? The sun and moon.'

These oral teachings are also named *symbola* meaning tokens of associations, serving, it is believed, as verbal checkpoints for the Pythagorean community. This especially makes sense for questions and answers, where one Pythagorean would ask the question, while the second would answer with the philosophical password.

Mystical Beliefs

Pythagoras most certainly believed in some form of reincarnation, which was determined by good and bad deeds. Convinced of the unity of living things, he once heard the cry of a puppy being beaten, to which he responded that the beating must stop, for he recognized the soul of his friend in the cry. Reincarnation as well was perhaps the latent supposition behind his saying that earthquakes are a meeting of the dead, and the reverberation of echoes were the voices of superior beings.

PHILOLAUS

Philolaus (*c.*470–385BC) was a later Pythagorean whose philosophy was in line or influenced by previous Pythagorean doctrine, but which resulted in an unexpectedly vibrant esotericism. As an elaboration on the Pythagorean notion that numbers constitute the universe, along with the doctrine of limited and unlimited, Philolaus posited a slightly different Pythagoreanism. He said that limiteds and unlimiteds, both now plural, harmonized the universe. His argument, although difficult to approach, suggests that, at bottom, things within the universe were both limited and unlimited, and consequently were in need of an explanation that involved both limit and the absence of limit. He also claims that all

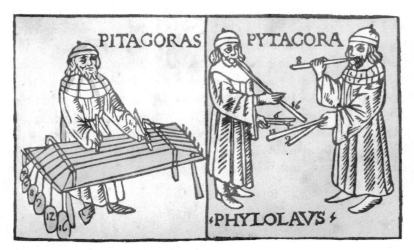

Philolaus was an esoteric philosopher who greatly expanded on the notion of the 'limited' and 'unlimited'

THREE KINDS OF PYTHAGOREANS

	GROUP ONE	GROUP ASSOCIATED WITH ALCMAEON	PHILOLAUS
PRINCIPLES OF UNIVERSE	The limited / odd and unlimited / even	The table of opposites	Limiteds and unlimiteds working in harmony

known things possess number, and furthermore there are not only even and odd, but a third, the even-odd. This is a good place to keep in mind that in Greek the words for 'odd' and 'even' are respectively, 'excessive' and 'complete'.

Harmony

Philolaus further makes the point that to understand the true nature of the limiteds and unlimiteds is beyond the scope of human knowledge. Yet we do have a certain knowledge of the universe and the things within it. If this is so, then the limiteds and unlimiteds must have been responsible for bringing the universe into being. Yet there remains a mystery: since both limiteds and unlimiteds have nothing in common, how could they have brought about the unity of the cosmos? Philolaus' answer is that there was a harmony which united them and allowed the arrangement of the universe. He implies that there was need of harmonization both between the unlimiteds and limiteds themselves and those things in the universe created and organized by them. For in the later case, the things brought into being by the limiteds and unlimiteds were as dissimilar to each other as well, and thus in need of harmony to arrange them.

Key points

- Early Pythagoreans were avid investigators of both mathematics and music and believed that number was the explanatory principle of the universe.

- Pythagoreans believed that number is directly responsible for abstract entities such as justice and reason and that all things in the universe exist as an imitation of number.

- One group of Pythagoreans believed in the odd and even as an underlying principle, which they considered the limited and unlimited, and another group of Pythagoreans adhered to the Table of Opposites, whereby the pairings of the Table are all related in some way.

- Pythagoras' teachings were passed down orally and can be divided into prohibitions, superlatives and definitions of things.

- Philolaus was a later Pythagorean who elaborated the notion of the underlying principle of numbers, and suggested that limiteds and unlimiteds, both concepts now plural, harmonized the universe.

Chapter 7

Heraclitus

AN UNORTHODOX MAN

In all the mysteries of classical philosophy, Heraclitus (*c.*535–475BC) might be the most enigmatic of them all. Dozens of his paradoxical sayings have been recorded. Even in antiquity, his ideas earned him the names 'riddler' and 'the obscure'. Like most Presocratic philosophers, understanding Heraclitus is difficult because of the metaphorical elements and terseness of his thought. Keeping in the tradition of the Presocratics, he divided his book *On Nature* into three parts: 'On the Universe', 'Politics' and 'Theology'.

Heraclitus was an enigmatic, combative philosopher who openly criticized the work of his predecessors

Heraclitus recognized that the reception of his arguments was influenced by his culture and predecessors. He openly attacked the prevailing authors of wisdom. Learning, he said, had not taught Hesiod or Pythagoras any sense. Pythagoras, according to him, was the chief of all imposters. Heraclitus was a distrustful man. He proclaimed that a fool loves to latch on to any news. Into this cultural mix, Heraclitus continued to challenge conventional wisdom. The religious oracle at Delphi was neither forthright nor coy, but gave signs requiring interpretation. Undoubtedly, it was this conception of wisdom, requiring effort by the interpreter, which prompted Heraclitus to write in his enigmatic style, 'The eyes are more accurate witnesses than the ears', because the nature of knowledge is to find out for oneself, not to lean upon the reports of others.

The Rational World

Heraclitus advocated that the world is rational and that man is a rational creature within it. A common element of understanding underlies everything, which he terms the *logos*. This is accessible to everyone, but seldom employed by the majority of people. Because of this ignorance, he compares their unawareness while awake to the insensible state of sleep. Heraclitus' philosophical insight is a striking one when first encountered.

Whether you walk up or down the path determines its nature and your destination

In Heraclitus' world, one principle is paramount: the unity of opposites. For example, disease is what makes health pleasant and good, just as hunger does to satiation, and fatigue is what makes leisure pleasurable. In the physical realm, the saying 'what goes up must come down' reflects this ancient wisdom. Heraclitus observed that cold things become warm, warm things become cold, the wet becomes dry, and the dry wet. Less obviously, he said that 'the way up is the way down', meaning that the way you go up a path is also the way you come down. There is only one path, but your orientation determines both the nature of the path and your destination. There is a natural connection and a

Heraclitus claimed that it was impossible to step into the same river twice, which was later popularized by Plato

relationship between things that appear to be opposed. While their opposition gives the appearance of separation and difference, deep down there is an order of unity.

Heraclitus describes this unity as 'god'. But unlike the doctrines of most religions, Heraclitus' god changes according to what pair of opposites he is, whether it is night and day or war and peace. There is a close association between the possession of a *logos* and the unity which is found so often in the world. With this background, more opaque thoughts such as, 'an unapparent harmony is stronger than an apparent one' and 'nature loves to hide' are made clearer by the recognition that there is a unity within the apparent disunity of opposition.

Heraclitus is probably best known for Plato's famous paraphrase: you cannot step into the same river twice. This thought suggests the transient nature of the world, but it also embodies Heraclitus' insistence that there is a greater unity in nature than in the currents of a river with which we happen to come into contact.

Heraclitus' understanding of the world is beautifully portrayed using the image of a bow or lyre, which has strings in tension with the rest of the instrument. Nevertheless, the production of harmony is only possible within the strain of this relationship, and it is the comprehension of this secret harmony that gives one the knowledge of the nature of the instrument. Even the most destructive force of all, war, can be called the father

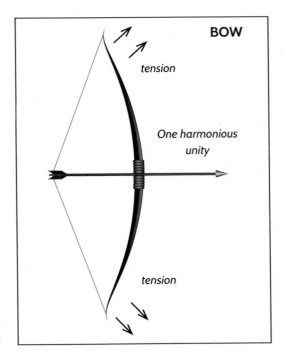

and lord of all things, because it is able to make some men free and others slaves and some cities prosper while others lie in ruins.

Opposition also exists in the animate world. The ass chooses the rubbish heap, rather than gold, for the pleasure of foraging, despite the apparent gap in worth between garbage and gold. Large grazing animals must be driven harshly by the whip to pasture. To put it another way, the pain of a beating leads to the pleasure of food. The pig would rather wallow in the murky slime of mud than be refreshed by the clear water of a well. The ocean, Heraclitus says, contains both the most polluted and most clean water. For it is poisonous to men, but is also essential for the fish that live within it. While the exact unity of these examples is sometimes hard to identify (just as one would expect for such 'unseen harmonies'), Heraclitus offered unique and paradoxical observations, which cohered within his framework of unity and opposition.

TABLE OF OPPOSITES

OPPOSITE	OPPOSITE	UNITY
Way up	Way down	Same road
Rubbish for ass	Gold for man	Worth
Day	Night	One day
Different waters	Different waters	Same river
Poisonous sea for man	Healthful sea for fish	Same sea

The Everlasting Fire

The character of the cosmos, in Heraclitus' estimation, is an 'everlasting fire'. The universe undergoes a cycle of being kindled and extinguished. Reminiscent of the role of air in Anaximenes' system, fire is the stuff from which all things are composed. The four elements of Greek philosophy (water, earth, air and fire) are closely linked and of these it is fire that plays the crucial role. Earth is created from the quenching of fire, and earth in turn can be melted by fire into liquid, which is nothing other than water. Evaporation, caused by the heat of fire, can also result in water. The primacy and potency of fire are at the centre of Heraclitus' understanding of the cosmos. To sum up this idea, he said, 'all things are in exchange for fire, and fire for all things'. This dependence may have been what he had in mind, along with notions of the divine, when he said, '[the]thunderbolt [considered as fire]steers all things'.

Heraclitus' astronomical explanations provided an ingenious synthesis of the observations available in his day. Fire was the elemental force in the universe and the sun and moon were round concavities, or bowls, the hollow core of which faced the earth. In each case, the concavity

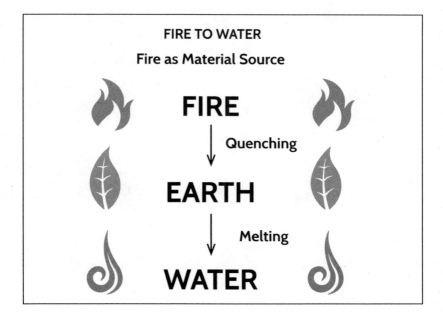

FIRE TO WATER

Fire as Material Source

FIRE

↓ Quenching

EARTH

↓ Melting

WATER

According to Heraclitus, the Furies were responsible for preventing the sun from overstepping its bounds

collects fire, which it then burns like a cauldron, the brighter and fiercer the closer it is to the earth, except for the moon, which possesses a lesser light because of its proximity to the limiting interference of the earth's atmosphere. Eclipses occur when the bowl's concavity faces away from us, while the phases of the moon are attributed to the burning bowl's gradual pivot away from our point of observation.

The sun was of particular interest, no doubt in part because of its fiery composition. Heraclitus made the seemingly bizarre claim that it had the width of a man's foot and that the Furies, the personified female avengers of Greek mythology, would keep the sun in check if it sought to overstep the boundaries of its orbit. Perhaps due to the nature of fire itself, which filled up the concavity of the sun, Heraclitus said that not only was the sun new each day, but it is always new without ceasing.

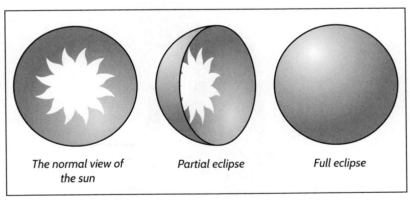

The normal view of the sun   *Partial eclipse*   *Full eclipse*

The Character of the Soul

As we have seen, Heraclitus had eccentric, though consistent and elegant, beliefs about the world, the heavens and the universe. The soul, in his scheme, also reflects the nature of the world and its fiery constitution. For example, he claimed that a dry soul is wisest and excellent. Perhaps he arrived at this belief because of the foolish behaviour of a drunk, whose soul, as if led by an immature boy, had been moistened. A wise soul, we may presume, has been properly dried out by fire in some manner or other. His account of the soul follows on naturally from his account of fire as the productive source of matter. That is, upon death the soul becomes water, while the 'death' of water is to become earth.

The explanation Heraclitus gives for human understanding and intelligence involves fire as well. During the day, the soul has direct access to fire, but at night, the people of the world must each kindle an inner fire as they sleep. Heraclitus' psychology, however, does not simply regard mental states as certain accumulations of fire without room for agency. A human is able to control mind and body to such a degree that Heraclitus famously said, 'Man's character is his destiny'. This encapsulates the idea that the world is comprehensible and accessible to the searching mind, yet this understanding must be one of an individual account, a *logos*, independent of the opinions of others.

For Heraclitus a dry soul represented wisdom and a wet soul, like that of a drunk, represented foolishness

Key points

- Heraclitus proposed the idea of *logos*, an intelligible understanding available in the world to everyone but taken up by only a few.

- Heraclitus' unity of opposites affirms that within the apparent hostility and opposition seen in the world, there is nevertheless a hidden unity.

- Heraclitus proposed that fire is a principle force in the eternal world and can transform to other elements, such as water or earth.

- The universe is a kind of everlasting fire, cyclically undergoing ignition and extinguishment, and astronomical observation could be explained in terms of fire: the sun, moon and stars were bowls filled with fire.

- The soul is either composed of fire or in close relation to it, a wise soul being dry, while a sleeping soul still has access to thought through an internally kindled fire.

Chapter 8

The Atomists – Leucippus and Democritus

Leucippus and Democritus

Leucippus (fl. 5th century BC) was the student of Zeno of Elea the student of Parmenides, and in turn he taught Democritus (b. 460BC). In an accident of textual history, we have a wealth of quotations and information about Democritus, but only a single quote from Leucippus: 'That all things come to be not by chance but by reason and because of necessity.' Therefore, we regard the words of Democritus as repre-

Leucippus left us only a single quote, but his faithful student Democritus brought his philosophy of atomism to a wider audience

sentative of Leucippus and also of atomism, to which they are jointly forever associated as founders. Democritus was a prolific writer, composing works on cosmology, sensation, logic and miscellaneous natural enquiries. There are various fanciful anecdotes about his life, but several sources seem to indicate that his death was precipitated by a period of voluntary starvation.

Plenum and Void

The philosophical background for Leucippus' atomism was the belief that, against the thesis of Parmenides, the universe was a plurality, and that things were in fact created and destroyed, opinions which generally

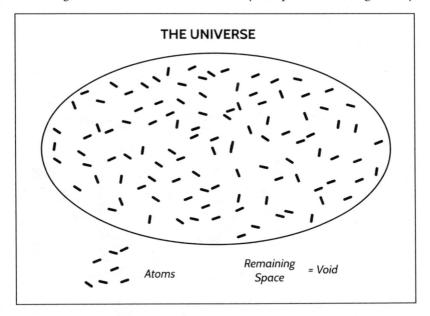

align with our everyday experience. The most detailed explanation of this philosophy is found in Aristotle, as is often the case with his predecessors. Aristotle tells us that at a most general level the fundamental nature of the world can be divided into the plenum (fullness) and the void.

In the plenum there are atoms, which come in an infinite variety and infinite quantity. The plenum can alternatively be considered simply as the atoms in distinction from the void. An atom is literally something that is 'uncuttable', as one should suppose the foundation stones of reality ought to be. The variations of the atoms amount to three kinds: shape, arrangement and position which are rather poetically termed 'rhythm', 'contact' and 'turning'. Just as Aristotle did using Greek, we can demonstrate these three kinds of variation with Latin letters as a stand-in for atoms. N differs from A in shape, while NA differs from AN in arrangement, and N from Z in position.

■ ATOMS DIFFER IN	
Shape, 'Rhythm'	as N to A
Arrangement, 'Context'	as NA to AN
Position, 'Turning'	as N to Z

A void was posited as a concession to the idea that in order to have motion, there must be space, or a void, within which motion for an object could take place. The void is non-existence or the lack of body or corporeality. A more abstract way of expressing it is that the plenum is 'what is', while the void is 'what is not'. Although the

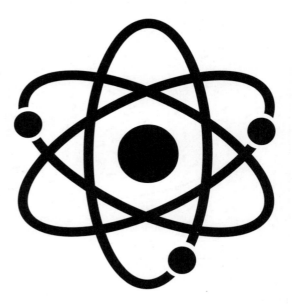

According to the atomists, the world is made up of small 'uncuttable' building blocks called atoms

universe is divided into the plenum and the void, it is itself infinite. A consequence of this idea was that the atomists also believed that there were a countless number of worlds in addition to ours.

In Atomic Detail

Atoms are in movement from mutual collisions. There is some testimonial evidence that this was affected by the weight of the atom pulling it in the appropriate direction. At any rate, it is by these motions of atoms that things come to be and are destroyed. The like are attracted

Atoms are attached to each other like hook and loop fasteners, and separate when forces are strong enough to tear them apart

to like atoms in the void, turning into a revolution, but when the number of them becomes too large, the finer of the atoms spin out to the edges. The result of such a process in the middle of this dense revolution is the creation of a world, such as our planet.

Atoms are all apparently made of the same kind of stuff; as a result, the bigger the atom, the heavier it is. Macroscopic beings, such as animals,

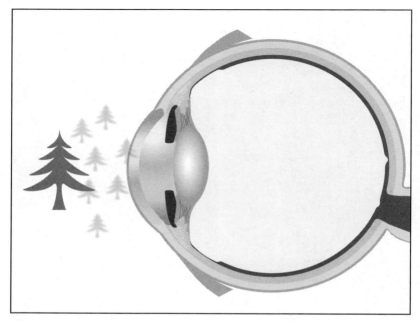

Eidola *were tiny images that emanated from objects and interacted directly with the eye*

plants or humans, are composed of certain conglomerations of atoms. The various shapes of the atoms accounts for the creation of these beings, with some hooked, or concave, or angular, and so forth. As a result, these atoms align in a similar fashion to hook and loop fasteners and likewise fall away when the forces of separation are sufficiently strong.

Perception

Democritus was an atomic fundamentalist. Even sight amounted to atoms coming into contact with one another. It was in this vein he said that, 'by convention, sweet, by convention, bitter, by convention, hot, by convention, cold, by convention, colour: but in reality atoms and void'. Whether touch, taste or sight, all these experiences of perception actually amount to little more than atomic motion. For sight at least, certain *eidola* or little images were believed to emanate from the objects of sight and directly interact with the eye. In fact, even the pleasures of the flesh were more alike than not, again being explained by a shared origin in atomic stimulation. Democritus said, with this similarity in mind, 'when people scratch themselves they are pleased in the same way in which those who are having intercourse are'.

Despite the confidence in the senses, which may be supposed to naturally accompany this corporeal theory of perception, Democritus was sceptical of the senses. He held this belief in part because the condition of the body was always in flux. Since this amounted to nothing more than a change in the constitution of atoms which compose the body, this necessarily alters the reliability of the perception.

The contrast between word and speech had great importance for the Greeks from the time of Homer

Democritus disparagingly referred to two kinds of perception, the 'bastard' and the 'legitimate', playing off a genealogical metaphor. To the bastard belong sight, hearing, smell, taste and touch.

Ethics

Considering Democritus' contributions to the history of atomism and his subsequent fame, it is surprising that the majority of his extant quotations concern advice on how to live. His incisive wisdom frequently appears to operate within the context of pairs of ideas, one of which is good, the other bad. The unwise and the wise, wisdom and fortune, action and words, need and luxury are some of the oppositions he uses.

Democritus often gives exhortations to wisdom, even though he may be less than precise about the details of such a life. He said, 'nature and teaching are neighbours. For teaching reshapes the person, and in doing so creates a nature'. It is probably this concept of a second nature

Democritus provided a wealth of advice on how to live

acquired by training that he has in mind when he says that nature is self-sufficient and exceeds the advantages of fortune. There are, however, advantages of fortune, but he draws a contrast between them and the fruits of wisdom: 'Those without understanding are shaped by the advantages of fortune, but those who have knowledge of such things are shaped by the advantages of wisdom.'

Another opposition in Democritus is that of word and speech, a contrast of much importance for the Greeks since the time of Homer.

■ PURPOSE IS BESTOWED ON THINGS BY US AND BY CHANCE		
	Value	Why
Water	good	for thirst
	bad	drowning
	good	swimming

'The word is a shadow of the deed' Democritus said, suggesting either that words are but an inert side effect of action or that, like a shadow, words necessarily mimic and follow the more substantial reality found in actions. Whatever the relationship, although actions can determine words to some extent, it cannot happen in reverse, 'a good word cannot deface a base action, nor can a good action be defiled by the outrage of a word'.

Ethics and Atoms

It is reasonable to suppose that the ethical theory of Democritus was influenced by his atomistic theory. Like the philosophy of Empedocles, the atomist theories were, at root, explanations that did not appeal to the gods, purpose or design. Because of this conviction, Democritus did not see in the objects around us meaning and purpose, but rather considered each thing in light of its usefulness, or not, to our needs. For example, he said that, 'from those things from which we get things good for us, we also find out things bad'. He continues on to explain that deep water is one such example. Water is good for us, but can also be bad, because we can drown in it. Yet in recognition of this we have learned how to swim, which is, in turn, a good thing for us. The determiner of whether something is good or bad for us is wisdom, which is the capacity to direct things to our own ends. It is this design, which the universe lacks, which we must instead infuse into our way of life. He was not inconsistent in the application of this worldview, even going so far as to recommend the use of house slaves as parts of the body, to whatever use they can be put.

In contrast, as we have seen above, those who refuse to learn the lessons of wisdom are at the mercy of happenstance – atoms twisting and turning in the void, a condition so common we have come to apply the name 'fortune', *tuche* in Greek, to it. While medicine was for the body, wisdom was for the maladies of the soul, both arranging their respective domains into an order the atoms are all too ready to dissolve. As we have seen in the creation of worlds, Democritus is committed to the idea that like attracts like. A similarity to this idea, imported into the realm of human behaviour, is that, 'continuous company with base men increases the state of evil'. On the other hand, he said, 'Being of one mind makes friendship'. The idea that like associates with like, whether directly owing to the interaction of atoms or not, also is developed in the idea that the effect of a thing is like its cause. Democritus applied this insight to the fact that when we observe noble deeds, great delights arise in us.

As much as Democritus advocated the cultivation of wisdom he acknowledged that in the face of our world of atomic flux, this is a difficult request. He advocated for the pursuit of a rigorous dedication to wisdom, because 'more people come to be good by practise than by nature'. He taught that in both success and failure there is toil, but it is only in success that the unpleasantness of toil is lessened.

Key points

- In Leucippus' concept of atomism, relayed through his student Democritus, there is the plenum, or atoms, what is; and the void, what is not.

- The void allowed for the possibility of motion for atoms, which are infinite and differ from each other in shape, arrangement and position, and which mechanically 'stick and fasten' to each other to create things larger than atoms.

- All perception is explained by one like atom coming into contact with another like atom; for example, the theory of vision involved the so-called *eidola*, little images, emanating off the object of perception and moving to the eye.

- The concept of opposition underpinned Democritus' ethical beliefs, such as emphasizing hard work, wisdom, action and need at the expense of their opposites, laziness, blind luck, words and luxury.

- Democritus' atomism influenced his ethics in that since atoms determined the reality of the world, there was no role for design or purpose and because the atomic world lacks purpose, reason must be used on things to benefit our own self-interest.

Chapter 9

The Sophists

The sophists were literally 'wise' or 'clever' men, their love of wisdom reflected in the root meaning of 'sophist', which also makes up part of the word 'philosophy': *philos* is Greek for 'loving' and *sophia* is Greek for 'wisdom'. As a group, they are often counted among philosophers because of their professed claims to knowledge as well as their very public disputes with Plato and Aristotle. There is no single reason as to why or how this group arose, but several causes seem to have been in play, including the lack of a consensus among Greek philosophers about what is ultimate reality; the ability to defend

Aristophanes wrote a play which depicted Socrates as a sophist

oneself in legal proceedings; and the need for a private educational market for Athenian youth. Socrates was notoriously prosecuted for, among other things, charging a fee for teaching. It is exactly this practice that the sophists proudly advertised, promising would-be students the ability to win an argument or persuade a crowd.

Philosophers and sophists were closely linked in the popular imagination, and it was at least credible for the Athenian playwright Aristophanes to write a play, *The Clouds*, which, to great comedic effect, portrayed Socrates as a sophist. Aristophanes and Plato both attributed to the sophists the practice of making the weaker argument stronger; that is, of two sides in a dispute, a sophist would take up the side with apparently less validity, credence or truth. Aristotle wrote a book, *On Sophistical Refutations*, with the aim of refuting the logical fallacies employed by sophists to win arguments. The sophists' antagonisms with Plato, Socrates and Aristotle gave rise to a reputation for relativism, opportunism and generally unprincipled 'sophistry'. In addition to the sophists' unfavourable link to philosophy, whose practitioners by contrast were often conceived as pursuers of truth, they were involved in a theoretical dispute about the law itself. The sophists called into question the distinction between, on the one hand, the law and custom and, on the other, nature, claiming this distinction was both artificial and contrary to nature.

PROTAGORAS

By far the greatest of the sophists were Protagoras and Gorgias, who are each represented in a Platonic dialogue of the same name. Despite this fame we have very few direct quotations from Protagoras himself, aside from the dialogue contrived by Plato for his own purposes. Protagoras (c.490–420BC) was the first sophist whom we know to have charged some type of fee for teaching and, additionally, he was the first to make the claim that he could make the weaker argument stronger. He wrote several treatises, which have only survived through the works of later authors, including *On Truth*. This work also gained the provocative title *Castings Down*, as a metaphor for wrestling moves that defeat an opponent, casting him on the ground. Although most of the curriculum remains a mystery, Plato's dialogue states that Protagoras taught his students the measured analysis of language, including interpretive work on poetry.

Man is the Measure

We possess two very intriguing and controversial claims from Protagoras, each of which did little to extinguish doubts of being a teacher of relativism. The first of these ideas is expressed in the following: 'Of all things man is the measure, of things that are, that they are, and of things that are not, that they are not'. Plato's understanding of this is that the standard of how things are in the world is a direct result of how we perceive things are. If the wind blows on you and on me and to me it feels cold, then it is cold; if it feels warm to you, then it is warm. Consequently, things in themselves are not absolute in a particular way, but are relative

89

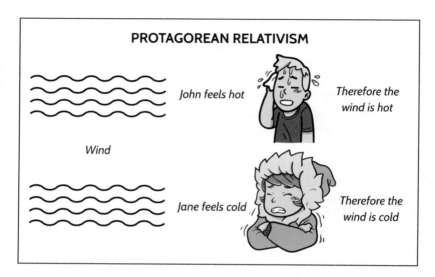

in the way that they are experienced by me, or by you, or by somebody else. This particular understanding of Protagoras' idea has often come to be referred to as Protagorean Relativism.

The Uncertainty of the Gods

In addition to this form of relativism, Protagoras also said that when it comes to the gods, he is uncertain as to whether they exist or not because of the unclarity of the issue and the briefness of human life. This agnosticism and his rather bold advertisement of the belief gave him a reputation of being an atheist while simultaneously making him vulnerable to charges of a mercenary intellect.

Teaching Virtue

Protagoras was among the first to claim to be able to teach virtue, *arête* in Greek, to his students. In fact, at the time this amounted to an education in the art of the political, a task less theoretical than pragmatic.

GORGIAS

Gorgias (*c.*483–375BC) was as important and as well known as Protagoras. He was from Leontini in Sicily but, like Protagoras, settled in Athens. He was reputed to have lived well past the age of 100, achieving a level

Gorgias attained such wealth that he could build a golden statue of himself at Delphi, the home of the oracle

of success sufficient to pay for a golden statue of himself at Delphi, the famous seat of the Greek oracle.

Gorgias believed that opportunity, the appropriate timing of persuasion, was critical for convincing others. Unlike Protagoras, he denied that he could teach virtue to his pupils. He was more dedicated to the art of rhetoric than other sophists, more given to awe and persuading crowds using novelties and coinages of speech. These included the rhyming of word endings, balancing sentence parts and using parallels and contrasts. One particular coinage he was ridiculed for was calling vultures 'walking coffins'.

On Nothingness

One particularly brilliant display of his oratory was a speech claiming that the universe is one, putting him in direct competition with philosophers such as Parmenides. In this speech Gorgias makes three claims: nothing exists; that if something did exist, we could not know it; and that even

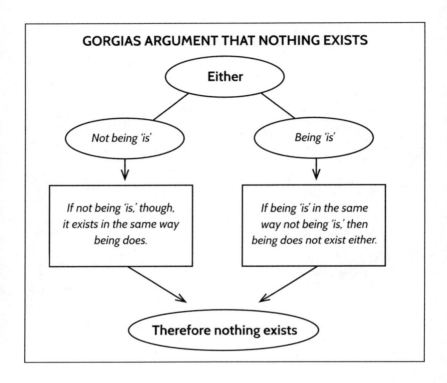

if it both existed and is known, it could not be communicated to others. Gorgias attempted to prove the first of these – nothing exists – by pointing out that many philosophers have disagreed among themselves. Some say the universe is one, others that it is many, while even others say it was created, and others claim it has always been. He makes a further point, perhaps merely semantic, by acknowledging not being, we are by virtue acknowledging being. Furthermore, if we say not being 'is' just as much as being 'is', then that means being is not. By this line of reasoning, Gorgias arrives at the incredible and crowd-inspiring conclusion that nothing exists.

PRODICUS

Prodicus (fl. 5th century BC) was an Athenian sophist, a figure about whom little is known, but who shows up in Platonic dialogues as a stereotypical expositor of the sophist's art. In one of the dialogues, the

Hercules was forced to choose between Pleasure and Virtue

Cratylus, Socrates gives a good-natured jab at Prodicus' tiered pricing for education, complaining that at 50 drachmas he could not afford the full treatment, so he made do with the one drachma speech instead. In another of Plato's dialogues, the *Euthydemus,* he is characterized as being mainly concerned with the correctness of names. Aristotle gives an example of this penchant when he says that Prodicus distinguished joy, delight and cheerfulness as different types of pleasure. One rather elaborate myth he composed saw Hercules visited by two nymphs, Pleasure and Virtue. The former offered him an easy and contented life, and the latter a hard and challenging path filled with glory. Hercules chose Virtue.

ANTIPHON

Antiphon, one of the more outspoken proponents of the division between human law and nature, wrote a book *On Truth*, which

93

Antiphon's book On Truth *is one of the few written fragments of the sophists to survive*

concerns both cosmology and anthropology. There is a report of him confronting Socrates about why, instead of living in rags and eating like a miser, he did not charge so much money as to make a decent living. Antiphon was said to have given up the composition of tragedies and the practice of politics, setting up a stall in the marketplace of Corinth to sell his services as a healer of those in pain.

His rhetorical style was said to be similar to that of Gorgias, such as his description of earthquakes as 'becoming wrinkled', in addition to various coinages attributed to him.

Antiphon set up a stall in the marketplace of Corinth where he worked as a healer

■ EXAMPLES OF SOPHISTIC COINAGE		
Sophist	**Term**	**Description of**
Gorgias	'living coffins'	vultures
Antiphon	'wrinkle'	earthquake
Prodicus	joy, delight or cheerfulness	pleasure

DISSOI LOGOI

This work is dated well past the classical period in Athens, the acme of sophistic activity, and is an accurate and fascinating record of the central idea of sophists: arguments can be defeated by arguments. This work, which can be called Competing Arguments, is a compendium of examples showing that in almost any arena of life an argument can be made on two sides. It begins by disputing the idea that there are good things and bad things.

A broken pot may be bad for its owner, but provides an opportunity for pot sellers

For example, a pot breaking is bad for the owner, but good for pot sellers. Victory is good for a winner but bad for a loser. In this manner, this small treatise goes through numerous examples, which lead to the same conclusion. The analysis too extends from the good and bad to the seemly and shameful, just and unjust, true and false, and so forth.

■ EXAMPLES FROM *DISSOI LOGOI*		
Situation	**Bad for whom?**	**Good for whom?**
worn out shoes	shoe owner	shoemaker
smashed ship	ship owner	ship builder
war	Persians	Greeks
sickness	patient	doctor

Key points

- Sophists were self-professed 'wise men' who made claims to be able to teach various practical skills, like virtue or politics.

- The sophists emerged out of the need for skilled legal defence, the seeming futility of philosophical argumentation and the lack of an educational market.

- The well-known sophist Protagoras claimed an ability to teach virtue and taught in exchange for money, impressing on his students an analytic mind for language of all sorts.

- Protagoras believed that man is the measure of all things, meaning that there is no truth in things themselves, but their value or meaning depends on the way they appear to us.

- Gorgias was reputed for his coinages, elaborate diction and clever reasoning and argued that even if something exists, we cannot know it, and even if we know it, we cannot communicate this to others, and therefore nothing exists.

- *Dissoi Logoi* or Competing Arguments is a Hellenistic-era document using examples to show that for all topics, pithy arguments can be made for both sides of most cases, whether good or bad, seemly or shameful, just or unjust.

Chapter 10

Socrates

Socrates (*c.*470–399BC) is the prototypical philosopher, a figure whom all previous philosophy seems to anticipate and all subsequent philosophy strives to emulate. In fact this characterization has been so influential, especially through Aristotle, who was the student of Socrates' student Plato, that Socrates' philosophical predecessors are called Presocratics.

Aristotle points out three things Socrates introduced into philosophy. The first is that he focused on ethical matters to the neglect of physical theory, second he sought the universal, and third he was constantly seeking definitions. This account generally accords with what scholars commonly ascribe to the early dialogues of Plato. In these early works, it's believed that Plato was depicting a Socrates more faithfully historical than the Socrates that emerges in later dialogues, a figure increasingly occupied by abstruse questions of

Socrates is the most famous of all of the classical philosophers and focused on ethical concerns

metaphysics and epistemology. Of course, Socrates never wrote anything, so everything that we know about him comes from a handful of contemporaries including Xenophon the historian, Aristophanes the comic playwright and Plato the philosopher, along with fragments from other authors and later anecdotes. Aristotle was two generations removed from Socrates, although still considered a valuable source. Plato is by far the most influential source for the Socrates of popular perception and Socratic philosophy. There is much scholarly dispute about the historical validity and various shadings Plato may have added to his portrayal of Socrates in his dialogues.

GUILTY OF PHILOSOPHY

In the *Apology*, which simply means legal defence in Greek, Socrates defends himself against charges of corrupting the youth, of neglecting the customary gods of Athens, and of introducing new gods. He is convicted and subsequently drinks hemlock as an enforced suicide. It is in the context of these charges that we will first engage with Socrates' public persona in the city of Athens.

Socrates committed suicide by drinking hemlock after his trial

Socrates was certainly not atheistical or irreligious. In several of the dialogues he objects to what he considers impious depictions of the gods: committing adultery, lying, murdering, with petty and jealous personal character. This reformed view of the gods was in conflict with conventional theology, influenced by the tradition of poets such as Homer and Hesiod, where infighting and adultery among the gods was commonplace.

Socrates was also charged as a teacher of youths who took payment for his teaching. Paid teaching was a feature of the sophists of the time, and would have associated Socrates with those unprincipled rhetoricians. Socrates, in his defence, points out by name several sophists who teach for money, while denying that he engages in such a practice. Socrates did in fact associate with the youth of Athens, although it is debatable whether he taught or merely conversed with them. Nevertheless, this apparent association with the sophists, no doubt reinforced by Aristophanes' play *The Clouds* wherein Socrates is depicted as a sophistical stargazer, did not help him in the courtroom. In addition to the formal charges, another aspect of Socrates' personality would have also given offence. This was his habit of meeting people in the marketplace of the city, pestering them with questions and often leaving them frustrated. It is to a more formal examination of this method of conversation that we now turn.

The Socratic *Elenchus*

Socrates sought definitions of things; above all, he looked for the definitions of moral qualities such as temperance, wisdom or justice.

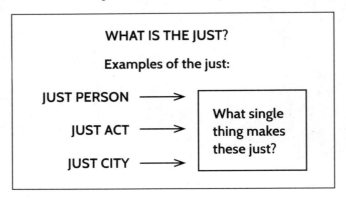

When he would enter into a dialogue with someone, he would ask, 'What is X?' In the case of the *Euthyphro*, the X is piety, in the *Charmides*, the X is temperance, and in the Laches, the X is courage.

Socrates expressed his philosophy through dialogues carried out between Athenian citizens

Can a rocking chair be a 'chair' if it does not possess four legs?

During these dialogues, Socrates would often try to refute his interlocutor, a process called the *elenchus*, meaning refutation in Greek. This process unfolds within the scope of a dialogue, which means that the give and take of conversation changes and influences the course of this refutation. Ostensibly, Socrates and his interlocutor, different in each dialogue, would pursue the definition of one of these moral qualities, such as courage. The definition of refutation in the case of the dialogues had a more broad meaning than the provisional sense of a refutation.

For example, imagine that Socrates asks John for a definition of chair. John replies that a chair 'is a piece of furniture with four legs'. Socrates examines this definition and asks whether a table is a chair, to which John says no. He then asks John whether a rocking chair is a chair, to which he says yes. Then Socrates points out that a table has four legs and is furniture, and that a rocking chair does not have four legs, but is nevertheless considered a chair. By the end of this exchange, Socrates has shown to John that the definition of a chair as a 'piece of furniture with four legs' is incompatible with John's understanding of a table and a rocking chair. Although a simplification, this is the basic way in which Socrates practises the *elenchus*.

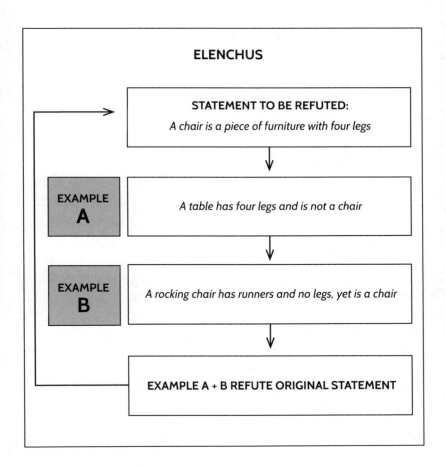

Virtue is Knowledge

As could be expected for someone who values the definitions of things, Socrates puts a premium on knowledge. Yet even though he values all knowledge, Socrates places ethical knowledge above all other kinds. Still, all the different types of knowledge of various human activities are related in that they confer an ability to be excellent in each of those respective activities. A person who knows geometry well, will be a good geometer. Socrates believed that, in a similar way, a person who knows about moral goodness, will be a good person. That is to say, simply knowing what is good is sufficient for, and necessarily leads to, being a good person.

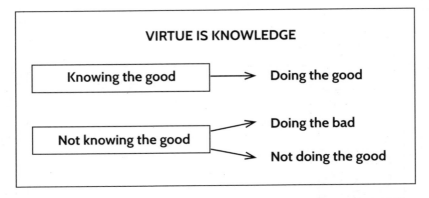

This knowledge is accompanied by a desire to do the right and an ability to accomplish the right, whatever that might mean in the circumstances. So then, to put it simply, Socrates' conviction is that to have knowledge of virtue is all one needs to be virtuous, and more forcefully, if one has knowledge of virtue, one is necessarily virtuous: virtue is knowledge.

No One Willingly Does Wrong

One of the problems for Socrates' view that virtue is knowledge is to explain why some people do not choose virtue. Certain people seem to willingly choose vicious actions instead of noble ones. However, Socrates does not agree that people willingly do wrong. No one acts in a way contrary to virtue as a willing party. The question then is how to explain behaviour that signifies people are willingly choosing the wrong action. Socrates' belief that virtue is knowledge means that as soon as this knowledge of virtue is possessed, the person willingly follows virtue. The implication of this is that ignorance, or lack of knowledge, is responsible for people choosing vice instead of virtue. The removal of this ignorance, that is, the acquisition of knowledge, causes people to be virtuous.

Socrates also insists that all men wish to be happy and not miserable. As a result, he believes that nobody will voluntarily pursue those actions, specifically vicious actions, which will lead to an unhappy life. So when people do in fact choose a life of vice, they are doing so because they believe that the actions that they are pursuing are good, even though they are not. In other words, they are pursuing the apparent, but not the actual, good. It is in this sense that no one willingly does what is wrong.

According to Socrates, no one willingly does wrong, but rather they commit evil acts out of ignorance

When people do wrong, it is because, due to ignorance, they pursue things that appear to be good, when in fact they are not.

The Unity of Virtues

In this discussion of the virtues, Socrates is often conceiving of the four Greek virtues: wisdom, temperance, justice and courage. Each virtue has the same aim, and because the object, the good, for each virtue is the same, Socrates is committed to say that the virtues are one. There is another way to make sense of this notion that the virtues are one; namely, that wisdom takes pride of place among the virtues. That is, if one is wise then one is, for example, also courageous, or has temperance, or is just. He might also be thinking of piety as well. Socrates subscribes to the common sense idea that each of these virtues promotes a happy life. However, unconventionally, he also believes that each of the virtues is a kind of knowledge. In thinking that each kind of virtue is a type of knowledge, Socrates evidently believes that in some sense each virtue seeks to lay hold of that which is good. If one does not know how to live temperately, then one is simply not wise. On the other hand, being courageous itself involves wisdom in the sense of involving judgement, discretion and understanding in cases of courage.

Key points

- Socrates' ideas survived through Plato's writings and mark a divide in philosophical investigations, with those before him or contemporaneous with him known as Presocratics.

- Unlike the Presocratics, Socrates focused on moral philosophy and sought out the essence of things through dialogues and a process of *elenchus* (refutation), whereby he attempted to make his interlocutors contradict themselves.

- Socrates believed that merely knowing what is good is sufficient to be virtuous and do the right thing; conversely, ignorance prevents pursuit of the right action or results in something other than the right action.

- All men wish for happiness and vicious actions, which lead to an unhappy life, come from ignorance because they erroneously appear to be the right choices.

- Socrates believed that each of the virtues – wisdom, courage, temperance and justice – is a kind of knowledge. Thus to possess wisdom is to possess all the virtues.

Chapter 11

Plato

Plato is arguably the most important philosopher of all time. Plato (c.423–347BC) founded and was the first head of the Academy, his school of philosophy, giving not only the modern world the notion of 'academic', but also the predecessor of the modern university. Plato was only in his twenties when Socrates died and this event was a lasting influence, not only as a dramatic feature, but also as philosophical fodder for the dialogues. Plato apparently borrowed the dialogue form from both tragic and comedic dramas, as well as from a semi-

Plato, the student of Socrates, set up the first school of philosophy in his Academy

comic genre of literature called a mime. Furthermore, there was in Plato's time a popular form of literature called 'Socratic Dialogues'; except for Plato we have mostly fragments of these from other authors, except for the historian Xenophon, whose writings include a collection of Socratic dialogues.

At any rate, for Plato the dialogue form can be filled with any number of characters, is often set in all kinds of locales, such as the gymnasia or someone's house, can contain a discussion about several or sometimes one topic, and usually has a dramatic date which differs from the date Plato composed it. With all these moving parts, the dialogue can often be a difficult place in which to sift out the philosophical meaning Plato intended. Most obviously though, Plato is speaking through the voices of his characters, so that it can be difficult to determine what conviction,

Xenophon was the only other writer than Plato to have recorded a substantial number of Socratic dialogues

if any, Plato has toward the opinion being espoused. Nevertheless, a number of topics and ideas are repeatedly stressed in the dialogues, often in the voice of Socrates, who can reasonably be said to be defending these ideas to some degree.

Plato's dialogues were often set at someone's house and could discuss a single topic or a multitude of issues

THE THREE-PART SOUL

In Plato's *Republic* a description of the human soul is given in which there are three parts.

To begin with, the soul is that which is not the body and is eternal. We are more truly our soul than our body. One part of the soul is called the 'appetitive'. To this part belong the bodily desires such as for food, drink and sex. A second part is the 'spirited'. To this part belong anger, courage and other passions. It perhaps could be considered the wilful part of our soul, but it is difficult to say because Plato said very little about the spirited soul. The last element of Plato's psychology was the 'logical'. It is the most important part, for, in a correctly ordered soul, it is this part that dictates thoughts and behaviours to the appetitive and spirited parts. Furthermore, it gives orders to the appetitive and spirited parts so that they are correctly working for the benefit of the whole person. It is the logical part of the soul that rules the other two by reason, deliberating for the benefit of the whole person in terms of the good and the beautiful.

ELEMENTS OF THE SOUL

LOGICAL

(seat of reason)

SPIRITED

(strong passions such as anger and courage)

APPETITIVE

(bodily desires such as food, drink and sex)

TWO WORLDS: INTELLIGIBLE AND SENSIBLE

Plato also divides up the world, or more correctly, reality, into two parts. There is the 'sensible' and the 'intelligible'. To the sensible belongs everything we can see, touch, feel and smell around us. It is the corporeal and embodied matter in which we live our day-to-day lives. To the intelligible belong only those things that can be metaphorically 'seen' or apprehended by the mind. The intelligible realm is more 'real' than the merely sensible. Furthermore, the sensible is dependent on the intelligible, which is explored in the next section.

The Divided Line

In the *Republic* Plato offers up an analogy of a geometric line to better explain the intelligible and the sensible realms, but, more importantly,

The sun can be used as an analogy for the 'Form of the Good' – it brings light to the landscape, but the landscape is not considered to be the source of light itself

the Form of the Good. This mysterious element of Platonic philosophy is not fully explained, but it performs at least two very important functions. The Form of the Good is responsible for the truth of the objects of knowledge and confers a power to know for those who know. Plato uses the sun as an analogy to explain the Form of the Good. The sun gives light to other things; it illuminates, for example, rocks, lakes, ground and trees, but they are not considered to be the sun nor are they sources of light. In this analogy, the Form of the Good is the sun.

The concepts of the intelligible and sensible realms are also expanded upon. The intelligible realm is divided into two, containing both mathematical and scientific truths and also the Forms, while the sensible realm is divided into material objects on the one hand and images and shadows on the other hand. Each of these four subdivisions has a corresponding human capacity of the mind to grasp hold of it. So now in the intelligible realm, (1) the Forms are grasped by understanding (2) mathematical and scientific truths by thought, while in the sensible realm, (3) material objects are grasped by belief and (4) images and shadows are grasped by representation.

Above this hierarchy is the Form of the Good, which is not only responsible for the actuality of the intelligible and sensible realms, but is said to be 'beyond being'.

THE DIVIDED LINE

	Capacity of Soul	Realm
THE FORMS	**UNDERSTANDING**	Intelligible
Mathematical / scientific truths	Thought	
Material objects	Belief	Sensible
Images and shadows	Representation	

The Theory of Forms

Just what Forms do and how they do it has been a topic of contention since the time of Plato. 'Form' in Greek is usually translated as either *eidos* or idea, each derived from the same word meaning 'to see'. The philosophical problem motivating the Theory of Forms seems to be the problem of knowledge. Plato thought that in our everyday interaction with things, that is, the sensible world, things were in a perpetual state of change. People, and animals more generally, grow old and die, plants wither and rocks erode. Nothing it seems is unaffected by the state of flux. For Plato, this posed a problem: how can one know anything if things are always changing? What is the thing I think I know, this body of mine, for example, if it is changing every day? Plato thought that there could be no knowledge of things in the sensible world. The Theory of Forms is, at least in part, an answer as to how knowledge is possible.

The world exists in a state of perpetual change – so plants, animals and men grow, obtain maturity, then wither and die

Plato refined his theories after debate with his students and colleagues

If something is changeless, and is changeless indefinitely, that is, eternally, then this would make it a good candidate for being knowable. The Forms, in Plato's philosophy, are eternal, changeless entities, from which particular things in the sensible world somehow derive their own being. That is, there is a Form of Beauty, Wisdom, Unity and so on. Each thing that is beautiful 'participates' in the Form with the property of beauty to the greatest degree possible. For example, a beautiful flower participates in the Form of Beauty, until that point when it either dies or is no longer beautiful. Anything that participates in a Form in this way is said to be a particular in this relationship. Forms are also said to be models or paradigms for everything that participates in them. Minimally this means that the particular imitates or is a copy of the Form.

It is believed that throughout the dialogues Plato came to modify his Theory of Forms in response to criticism and reflection. Some of these changes may have included a reduction of the number of Forms, previously infinite, and elevating the importance of the Form in the Form–particular relationship.

Recollection and Reincarnation

Plato was committed to reincarnation. One reason he believed in reincarnation was due to the process of learning, which he did not, strictly speaking, consider the acquisition of something new, but rather the recollection of knowledge acquired in a previous life. One of his arguments begins by comparing two sticks, which we say are 'equal'. But no matter which two sticks we get, they can never be perfectly equal. That is, we compare them to the Form of Equal, and these two sticks are equal to each in an inferior manner, though the Form of

These two sticks may be described as 'equal' but when compared to the Form of the Equal they fall short

Equal is actually equal. Yet from our birth we are able to make these kinds of judgements involving the Form of Equality or Beauty or Just. So this indicates that we did not learn about these Forms, since we have seemingly always had them from birth. In Plato's explanation, we are simply recollecting the Forms from a previous life, comparing the Forms to their imperfect particulars.

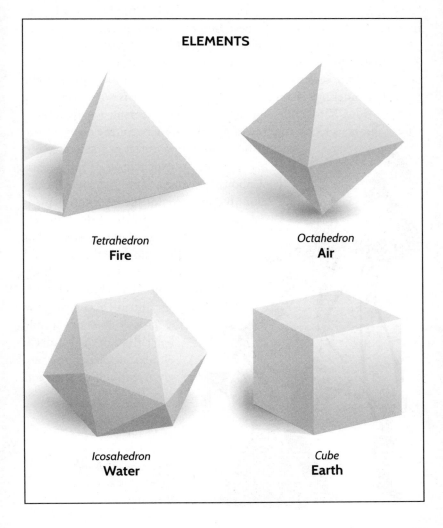

ELEMENTS

Tetrahedron
Fire

Octahedron
Air

Icosahedron
Water

Cube
Earth

The Physical World

Although the creation and makeup of the universe seems to hold a place less important than the intelligible world, Plato in later years wrote about it in the *Timaeus*. In this work, he posited that a demiurge, or divine craftsman, fashioned the world by looking to the Forms. He crafted the universe to be supremely beautiful because he is supremely good. The world is a kind of living creature with its own world-soul. The universe is itself spherical, the most perfect shape, while little bodies compose the matter of the universe. These bodies are geometrical shapes. For instance, water is made of isocahedrons and ether of pyramids.

Into this discussion, Plato introduces a strange idea, which has come to be called the receptacle. This receptacle is a kind of substratum; the thing that undergoes changes as a change occurs. That is, when something changes from X to Y, the substratum is that element, whatever it is, which allows us to say that the same thing underwent the change from X to Y. A final interesting aspect of the dialogue is that teleology, or an explanation of purpose, is continuously invoked. The craftsman brings about the universe for the best, and man, as a macrocosmic exemplar of the universe, shows the design of the universe. His head is the pilot of the soul and therefore at the top of the body and round. The chest holds the more estimable feelings, while the grosser passions reside beneath it, in the stomach. Similar explanations are given for the organs and even the soul.

In the Timaeus, *Plato argued that a divine craftsman made the world by looking to the Forms*

Key points

- Plato believed that the soul is divided into three parts: the logical, containing reason and, in a well-ordered soul, controlling the other two parts, the spirited, the seat of anger and passions, and the appetitive where bodily desires such as food, drink and sex reside.

- Reality is divided into the intelligible and the sensible realms; the former realm into Forms (including the Form of the Good) and mathematical and scientific truths, and the latter into material objects and images/shadows.

- The Form of the Good explains the existence of things that are known and those who know these things, in the same way that the sun both illuminates things and gives the light by which those things are seen.

- The Theory of Forms addresses the problem of knowledge when things seem to be in constant flux; particulars like a beautiful flower participate in the Form of Beauty, whereas the Form possesses the property perfectly.

- Plato believed in reincarnation, and that we recollect rather than acquire knowledge; that we have latent within us knowledge from a previous life, allowing us to compare things to the Forms.

- In the *Timaeus*, Plato's work on the physical world, a divine craftsman shapes the world; throughout the dialogue both the universe and man, a microcosm of the universe, are described in terms of design and purpose.

Chapter 12

Aristotle

Aristotle (384–322BC), the pupil of Plato, was a philosopher who made pioneering, influential discoveries and had strong opinions about biology, logic, physics, rhetoric, politics, ethics, theology, psychology, metaphysics and other areas. After studying for the better part of 20 years under his master Plato, Aristotle, perhaps expecting to be appointed the next head of Plato's Academy, was passed over for Plato's nephew, Speussipus. After this, Aristotle left the Academy and formed his own school, the Lyceum. The grounds of the Lyceum had a natural walkway, which is why

Aristotle was a student of Plato and formed his own school, the Lyceum

Aristotle and his disciples came to be called Peripatetics, deriving from the Greek verb for 'walk around'.

We do not possess all of Aristotle's work; reasonable estimates are that we have only around one-fifth of his original output. While Plato has cultivated a reputation as one of the most stylistically pleasing authors, Aristotle has dense prose. This is due in large part to the fragmentary nature of most of the works that have survived, likely parts of lecture notes or drafts, which, to understand properly, must often be supplemented with assumptions from his previous work or conjectural beliefs we attribute to him.

Speusippus, not Aristotle, was Plato's successor as the head of the Academy

He was a systematic thinker, which complemented this engagement with so many diverse fields of human knowledge. Much of his philosophy was in response to and sometimes at odds with his teacher Plato. In light of his emphasis on the here and now, he is often considered the philosopher of common sense. This reputation was justly earned, for Aristotle often sought to preserve the phenomena, that is, he looked for ways of explanation which tended to support how things appeared to be. This is in contrast to Plato, who sought for the true reality of things because he believed this world to be in an unknowable state of change.

In addition to his phenomenological conservatism, Aristotle's method also often includes two other features. The first is that he surveyed common opinions, either of the populace or of influential figures, both to comment on what they got right and wrong, but also to build on their contributions. The second is that Aristotle proceeded on a given topic by attempting to answer the questions arising from puzzles or difficult features of the particular field he was investigating.

THE FOUR CAUSES

The four causes, sometimes better understood as four explanations, are part of a conceptual framework for explaining how things come to be. The causes are brought up in Aristotle's *Physics*, where he introduces the concept of cause by contextualizing it using the question, 'Why?' Causes are explanations or answers as to why something has come about in the way it has. These causes have conventionally come to be called in English, material, efficient, formal and final causes.

The material cause is perhaps the easiest cause to remember and is the base material from which something is made; for example, if we have a bronze bust of Churchill, we know that the material cause is bronze. To put it another way, the statue consists of or is made of or comes from bronze.

The efficient cause is that which has initiated the change to bring about something into the state it is in. In the case of the bust, it is to assign the force which cast the bust into the bronze shape it is in now. Thus the sculptor and the tools of casting are the efficient cause of the bust.

The formal cause is the form or shape something takes, or more

THE FOUR CAUSES

1. Material Cause

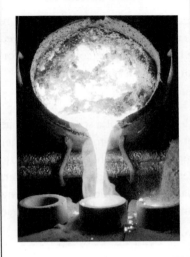

2. Efficient Cause

3. Formal Cause

4. Final Cause

IN HONOR OF THE PRIME MINISTER OF OUR FINEST HOUR

abstractly, the definition of a thing. In the case of the bronze bust, the formal cause is all its particularity including the erudite scowl of Churchill. The shape, form or definition that the bust has taken on is of Churchill's head.

The final cause is, in Aristotle's formulation, 'that on account of which'. Often this can simply be reduced to the purpose, or sometimes conceived of as the end or goal. In the case of the bust, it could be conceived as 'for' either decoration or commemoration of Churchill's tenure.

TEN CATEGORIES

In his little book *The Categories* Aristotle makes use of a scheme which he says applies to 'things which are'. It is not clear how Aristotle came to either the number ten or these categories in particular, but they probably arose as ways of asking a question about something. The categories are in order: substance, quantity, quality, relative, place, time, position, having, acting upon, and being affected. We may assume that Aristotle thought of these

■ ARISTOTLE'S CATEGORIES		
Example	Category	Answers the Question
horse	substance	What is it?
two feet	quantity	How much / long / high / big?
white	quality	What kind?
half	relative	As relates to what?
in the marketplace	place	Where?
yesterday	time	When?
sitting	position	In what configuration?
has shorts on	having	With what?
cutting	acting upon	What is it doing?
being cut	being affected	What is being done to it?

ten as irreducible and exclusive categories of how things are and how to describe them. For example, if we were to ask what something is, we would appeal to the category of substance to answer, for example, 'it is a horse'. If we were to ask 'how high is it?', we would answer using the domain of quantity and might say 'two feet'. And for the other categories he gives examples as follows: of quality, 'white', of relative, 'double' or 'half', of place, 'in the marketplace', of time, 'yesterday', of position, 'sitting', of having, 'has shoes on', of acting upon, 'cutting or burning', of being affected, 'being cut or being burned'. In short, beings are categorized into irreducible kinds that are mutually exclusive and for the most part answer, by classification, any question we can have about something else.

THE SOUL

The notion of Aristotle's soul (*psyche*) is difficult to understand, because it is a marked departure from the modern spiritualist idea associated

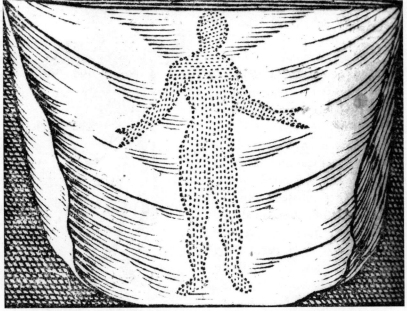

Aristotle saw the soul as essentially life, and, according to him, plants, animals and humans all possessed souls

with doctrines of the afterlife. For Aristotle it was essentially life and therefore it should be no surprise that, although he attributes different functions to each, Aristotle thought that plants, animals and humans alike have a soul.

When focusing on the human soul, and distinguishing between body and soul, Aristotle says that the soul is not body. The soul is actuality while the body is potentiality. This is consistent with the general understanding that, for Aristotle, matter is only potentially something; for example, the bronze that is transformed into a bust, while the soul is itself a potentiality; for example, the completed bust is the actuality of the bronze. Soul is the organic principle by which the body is organized and within which its faculties operate. Thus the soul is the actuality of a body with the capacity to function in the way a human body does.

ETHICS

Ethics or how to live was an abiding concern for Aristotle as it was for most classical philosophers. He set forth his views in the *Nicomachean Ethics*, a work possibly named for either his son or father, Nicomachus. Aristotle believes that people seek the best for their lives, a notion broadly given the Greek name *eudaimonia*, meaning 'favoured by the gods'. This understanding is sometimes glossed with the word 'flourishing', but can also be understood as happiness, refined and qualified in a particularly Aristotelian way. The candidate for this happiness, on Aristotle's reckoning, is something that we choose for its own sake – we do not choose to attain something

Aristotle's concept of happiness was eudaimonia, *and he believed all other virtues existed only to help us be happy*

Ethics was an overriding concern for Aristotle and he taught these ideas to major leaders such as Alexander the Great

further or beyond it. Additionally, this happiness must also serve as the end for all other goods. That is, all other goods, including both intellectual and ethical virtues, must be for the sake of this happiness. That is, we are just or wise or magnanimous in order, ultimately, to be happy, and having attained this happiness, we do not seek something beyond happiness. A complete account of this happiness includes that it is a virtuous activity of a life characteristically virtuous, guided by a rational intellect, not living the virtues by mere luck. Thus the virtuous life is a state or condition achieved by a life appropriately trained by habits.

THE MEAN

In the case of every virtue, there is a mean between two extremes. For example, when it comes to fear, there are two extreme conditions we can be in, rashness or cowardice. Rashness is extreme by excess, while cowardice is extreme by deficiency. However, courage is the mean, the ideal condition, between rashness and cowardice. Thus there is a pair of extremes for every virtue and an ideal mean to which the virtuous adhere.

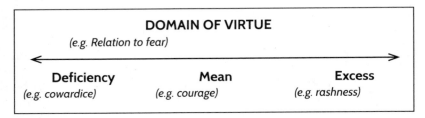

DOMAIN OF VIRTUE
(e.g. Relation to fear)

Deficiency	**Mean**	**Excess**
(e.g. cowardice)	*(e.g. courage)*	*(e.g. rashness)*

Aristotle identified three types of government, each with a good and deficient version – rule by one (monarchy/ tyranny), rule by the few (aristocracy/ oligarchy) and rule by the many (polity/democracy)

POLITICS

Aristotle's work *Politics* presents his views on the science of politics. His study of politics began when he and his students collected the constitutions, or plans of governments, from various city-states in Greece. Just as, in the case of the bust, the formal cause was the particular statue that it is, and for human beings, the formal cause is the soul, for the city-state, the formal cause is its constitution. The constitution, so understood, is not a written document, but rather the organizing ideas or principles that legislate and order the people into a city-state. Just as the individual has in mind the good life and happiness as the ultimate goal, the city-state has the same aims.

In Aristotle's judgement there are three types of government: one ruler, few rulers or many rulers. But for each type there is a good version and a deficient one. For one ruler, the good version is monarchy, while the deficient is tyranny. For few rulers, the good version is aristocracy

and the deficient version is oligarchy, and for many rulers, the good version is a polity and the defective form of government is a democracy. In Aristotle's view, the best constitution among these was the monarchy or aristocracy, where either the best man or men deliberated for the overall benefit of the city-state.

TYPES OF GOVERNMENT

	ONE RULER	FEW RULERS	MANY RULERS
GOOD	Monarchy	Aristocracy	Polity
DEFICIENT	Tyranny	Oligarchy	Democracy

Key points

- Aristotle defended common sense and sought explanations that preserved the way things appear to be; he surveyed opinions on a topic and directed his work to answering difficulties about a topic.

- Aristotle's four causes are material, efficient, formal and final; for example, in a bronze bust, the bronze is the material cause, the sculptor is the efficient cause, the shape in which the bust is cast is the formal cause and the purpose for which the bust was made is the final cause.

- The ten categories are irreducible things classified by reference to the kinds of questions which can be asked of them; they are substance, quantity, quality, relative, place, time, position, having, acting upon, and being affected.

- All living things have a soul, which is distinct from a body; the body has potential while the soul is the actuality of the living creature with the actualized set of capacities to live in a certain way.

- The goal of life is to achieve *eudaimonia*, a life blessed, happy and flourishing, and for this one must cultivate virtue in accordance with reason seeking the good; for every virtue there is both an excess and a deficiency, and one ought to strive for the mean between these extremes.

Chapter 13

Philo of Alexandria

Among the Hellenistic Jews of this period the most prominent and systematic is Philo of Alexandria. Philo (20BC–c.50AD) was a Jew of the diaspora living in Alexandria, Egypt, well educated and from a wealthy family. He spent his whole life in Alexandria, visiting the temple in Jerusalem only once. As the Hellenisation of the known world continued after Alexander the Great's death, this cultural influence also extended to religious belief. One of the more interesting manifestations of this interaction was the joining together of Judaism and Greek thought. One factor which made Greek thinking attractive to Jewish intellectuals of the time was a need to interpret the books of Moses in a non-literal fashion, a parallel precedent for which had been set out in the Greek allegorical interpretation of Homer. This earlier scholarship is important for understanding the context of such

Philo of Alexandria was a Jewish philosopher who used the discipline to better understand the Old Testament

Many Jewish intellectuals turned to Greek thought to find a way to interpret the books of Moses in a non-literal manner

Abraham featured heavily in Philo's writing and he used his philosophy to help answer complex theological questions

interpretation: in both the case of Homer and the Old Testament, this method of understanding is meant to more deeply bring out the meaning of the author, not to explain it away or alter it. Another motivation for the synthesis of Hebrew and Greek thought was, for those sufficiently cultured in the philosophy of the Greeks, certain perceived tensions between the Greek and Hebrew conception of reality. Was God completely transcendent, as Aristotle believed, or was he the personal God of Israel? Was the body tainted in some way, as Plato seemed to uphold, or did the God of nature deem the body, like all of creation, good?

It is Philo, if anyone, who exemplifies the creativity and syncretic pull of Hellenistic Judaism. A large part of his development was self-professedly a result of his early contemplative love of philosophy. Writing in Greek, Philo had a particular eye for religiously motivated questions, often orienting his work to disputes or questions about the books of Moses. In this vein he wrote *On Abraham*, *On the Life of Moses*, and *Questions and Answers on Genesis*. His other works are often divided into his more strictly philosophical work, and outwardly directed treatises with an apologetic tone.

In addition to offering us insight into philosophical developments of the time, Philo is also valuable because he represents an entrance point to understanding the greater intellectual atmosphere of the era, including the Judaism of the time and the Greco-Roman setting for the New Testament. Throughout his works there are traces of the influence of many Greek philosophies, including Epicureanism, Stoicism, Scepticism, Aristotelianism, and, especially, Platonism.

PHILO'S ALLEGORICAL INTERPRETATION

It is in the context of defending Judaism, either from internal discrepancy or from hostile criticism, that Philo embarked on his exegetical works, whenever possible attempting to preserve the literal truth of the books of Moses, but when such literalism is impossible, offering some symbolic interpretation. In light of this type of orthodoxy, it should be no surprise

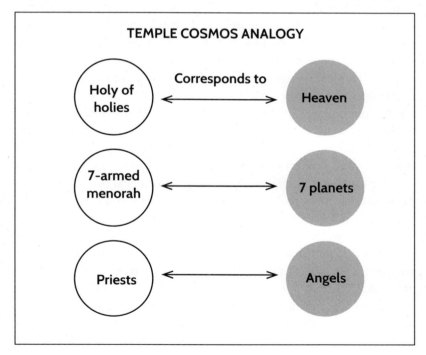

According to Philo, the sacrificial systems of the Jews and the Greeks closely corresponded to one another

that Philo did not think that philosophy was on a par with scripture. Rather, scripture, understood as divine wisdom, has philosophy as its maidservant, just as the process of education is the maidservant of philosophy. Often Philo's allegorical symbolism appeals directly, not only in method, but also in content, to Greek philosophical considerations. For example, when discussing the Jewish temple Philo says that the real temple is the universe, the holy of holies is the heaven, the seven-armed menorah is the system of seven planets, and the priests are the attendant angels of God. He continues on, occasionally in minute detail, as to the rest of the significations of the temple.

Although Philo sometimes assimilates the Hebrew tradition cleverly to the Greek, at other times he's interested in preserving the unique claims of the Jewish religion. One might immediately suspect, in this regard, a great similarity between the sacrificial systems of the Greeks and the Jews. Not so, claims Philo, because, for instance, in Genesis 15 Abraham makes a sacrifice of ox, goat, sheep, dove and turtledove. The ox corresponds to earth, the goat to water, the ram to air, the dove to the planets and the turtledove to the stars. Yet, although he believes this interpretation to be more in line with the textual context, Philo also has another understanding of the sacrificial, which is more closely symbolic of human concerns.

In this interpretation, the ox is related to the human body, for we must subdue and domesticate our body to the headship of the soul. The goat is similar to our sense perceptions, the turtledove to the faculty of

DOUBLE INTERPRETATION OF SACRIFICIAL SYSTEM

	COSMIC	HUMAN
Sacrificial Animal	Ist level explanation	2nd level explanation
ox	earth	human body
goat	water	sense perceptions
turtledove	stars	faculty of reason

reason, and other animals are all likewise explained in terms of human composition.

PHILOSOPHICAL THEOLOGY

Philo's theology was no less orthodox than his biblical interpretations, and here too he employed philosophical categories to express his beliefs. God was transcendent and no part of the created order, while the created order, including the stars and other celestial bodies, often deified by the Greeks, were brought down to the status of created things. Due to the nature of God as wholly other, Philo, in the tradition of Greek discourse about being and reality, describes God as that type of substance which truly exists. When Moses asked God to show himself, there was no sense organ that could have perceived him or any expectation that the mind could conceive of him. Because of this, Philo argues, God shows himself to be invisible and incorporeal, which also means humans can never attain knowledge of the divine essence. Although we cannot come to know God directly, we can approach and achieve partial knowledge through his powers.

The *Logos*

When it comes to God working through his powers, it is the Word (*Logos*) that mediates these powers. Philo's description of the Word is a near personification; the Word is the first born of God's sons, the eldest among the angels. In addition to the Word, he is called the First Principle and Likeness of God. The intermediary and instrumental nature of the Word is memorably explained by Philo as a rudder used by the captain of the universe to steer all things.

Because of the nature of the Word in its role as 'rudder' and first born of the universe, many have taken it to occupy a position halfway between the divine and the created. There is language that seems to both elevate the Word to the station of God and also to describe it as something created and subordinate. Further descriptions of the Word seem to openly, and creatively, borrow from Platonic theoretical philosophy. The Word is described as the shadow of God, which in turn serves as a further archetype for levels of creation beneath it. As if a craftsman, or to use the Greek word, a demiurge, the Word creates things and imprints them with its own seal. Man, in this scheme, is a reflection of the cosmos, or universe, just as the cosmos is a reflection of the Word. In a theological twist on a Platonic theme, Philo divides the universe into the intelligible and the sensible. The intelligible is the realm of God and angels, while mankind and the physical universe reside in the sensible realm.

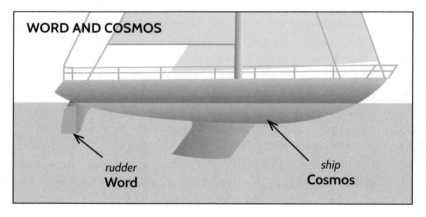

WORD AND COSMOS

rudder
Word

ship
Cosmos

Mankind

Just as ancient thinkers, especially Plato, conceived of the individual as a microcosm of the world and the world as a macrocosm of man, Philo also had his own perspective on this relation. In the universe composed of two parts, the intelligible realm precedes the sensible world. In a person, the divine creation of man as a likeness of God is of greater significance

The 'intelligible' was the realm of God and the angels alone, while the 'sensible' was the world of man

than the body of man, formed from the earth. The distinction made by Philo is not, however, as we might expect between soul and body. Rather the distinction for Philo was between the mind or intellect (Greek *nous*) and body (Greek *soma*). This certainly corresponds to the analogy of the universe: just as the Word guides the universe, so the mind guides a human body.

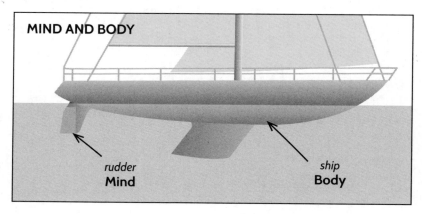

MIND AND BODY

rudder
Mind

ship
Body

PHILO'S ETHICS

Philo's ethical system adopted the Greek list of virtues: wisdom, temperance, justice, and courage. More specifically he advocated the model of a wise man, after the Stoic sage, who could so order his life as to live in imitation of God. However, there is a noticeable shift of emphasis from the Stoic system, from focusing on the sage as person, to an admiration and imitation of God as an exemplar for both sage and everyone else. In this sense, God was to be emulated because of his inability to be moved by the irrational passions such as sorrow or fear. Instead of passion, one should be ruled by reason in which there is a life free from trouble.

Key points

- Philo, a Jewish philosopher, represented the growing influence of Hellenistic culture and the perceived intellectual reconciliation that had to occur between Greek ideas and Judaism.

- Philo's work concerns the Hebrew scriptures and he appealed to symbolism whenever a literal interpretation seemed impossible, employing allegory to explain, for example, the symbolic meaning of the Jewish animal sacrificial system.

- God for Philo is a wholly transcendent, true being, existing in a way that cannot be fathomed by the human mind, but who works his powers through the *Logos* or Word, which, as an instrument of divine power, Philo describes in a metaphor as being the 'rudder of the universe'.

- Philo believed that the mind was created with a priority over the body, just as, in the universe, the intelligible realm of spiritual entities has priority over the sensible realm of matter.

- The cosmos or universe is but a reflection of the Word, while mankind is, in turn, a reflection of the universe.

- In light of the four Greek virtues, the sage should be followed as a model who himself has sought to imitate the example of God.

Chapter 14

The Sceptics

As a philosophical attitude, the seeds of scepticism were sown before full-blown scepticism came to the fore as a school of thought. Beginning with Socrates' persistent but often inconclusive questioning and his dictum that he knows that he knows nothing, we then see his disciple, Plato, cast doubt on the reality of our world, instead appealing to a world of Forms and immutable eternality. Even more sceptical are the sophists, whose beliefs and practices seem centred on the pragmatic concerns of financial and political success at the expense of convictions about the world.

In Greek philosophy there are two main variants of scepticism. One is Academic Scepticism, so-called because the inheritors of Plato's Academy eventually became adherents of a sceptical position for an extended period of time. The other is Pyrrhonian Scepticism, named after Pyrrho (c.365–270BC), the founder of a philosophical school.

ACADEMIC SCEPTICISM

Seventy-five years after the death of Plato, Arcesilaus became head of the Platonic Academy. Despite the Academy's tradition of developing and refining the Platonic system, Arcesilaus instead focused attention on making arguments that could support both sides of a question.

Academic Scepticism cannot be divorced from both the historical philosophical context and the contemporary climate where certain philosophies were dogmatically propounded, most notably in the systematic defence of Stoicism. Although sense impressions were supposedly always reliable, Arcesilaus conceived of two situations when duplicates or counterfeits of the real thing could fool impressions. The first example is mistaking one egg for another, or anything which is sufficiently similar, such as mistaking a twin, John, for his brother, James. In fact we can even extend this idea to artificial versions of reality, such as mistakenly biting into a wax apple. The second example of such illusion is a dream. When in a dream we may experience all kinds of impressions of sights, sounds and smells not of the wrong things, but of nothing at all.

Arcesilaus further advocated a suspension of belief, but it is unclear whether this meant that he advocated knowledge was not possible in some sense or merely that within some philosophical systems the claims for knowledge were inadequate.

Carneades

Carneades (c.214–129BC) led the Academy after Arcesilaus and, like him, followed Socrates as a model of someone who pursued the truth while coy about his own beliefs. The most famous anecdote about Carneades is that he was sent on embassy to Rome where he argued in favour of justice one day, and on the following day presented arguments against it.

Carneades was happy to argue in favour of justice one day, and against it the next

Even after acknowledging the acuity of sceptical arguments against knowledge, there was still a need to lead daily life and, more importantly, to attempt a life of happiness. To this end, Carneades advocated the adoption of the principle of the probable or to pithanon. Specifically in the case of perception, Carneades allowed that we should be convinced by impressions that are plausible or convincing, even though these in

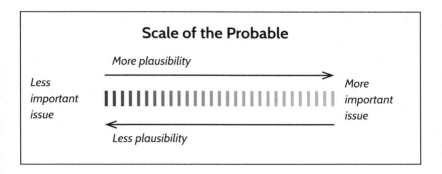

Scale of the Probable

More plausibility

Less important issue

More important issue

Less plausibility

fact may be wrong. The plausibility of an impression is scaled: we may take a lower standard of plausibility for those things of relatively less importance. For more important matters, the threshold for conviction is much higher.

Philo of Larissa

After the developments of Carneades, Philo of Larissa (*c.*154–84BC) further revised the sceptical approach. Philo believed that perceptions, at least some of them, are probably true. This tepid endorsement of perception was in the context of continuing disputes with Stoicism. He deployed Stoic argumentation against its own school, beginning with the idea that the sage, the ideal Stoic wise man, never assents to non-cognitive impressions. (A cognitive impression is one that informs us about the content of the world or some aspect of the way the world exists, such as the way perception represents, for example, an apple. A non-cognitive impression is one that does *not* give information about the world.) That left only the category of cognitive impressions to which one could give assent, but

The wise man should never assent to impressions that do not give information about the world

Philo believed he had shown that cognitive impressions do not exist. So, since cognitive impressions do not exist and non-cognitive impressions should never be assented to, the proper attitude we are to take is one of sceptical withholding of belief.

Rather than gradually passing away, the decline of the Sceptical Academy came about when Antiochus, a new head of the Academy, took over, essentially returning the school to an earlier form of Platonic dogmatism.

PYRRHONIAN SCEPTICISM

Pyrrho (c.365–270BC), the founder of the school of scepticism, began his career as a painter. If the anecdotes about him are to be believed, he was equally indifferent to both the affairs of the world and to goings-on about him. In fact, because of this attitude, friends would follow him as he went about his daily life, at least once saving him from the oncoming danger of a wagon. Once, on a boat in the middle of a storm, Pyrrho pointed out to others a pig blithely continuing on its meal. This ought to be the life of a wise man, he told them, like a pig indifferent to a storm. Although the accuracy of these stories might be in doubt, to some degree they demonstrate that, even if Pyrrho's scepticism was not so extreme, he was thoroughly committed to scepticism as an influence on his actions as well as on his thoughts.

Pyrrho (c.365–270BC) founded the school of scepticism

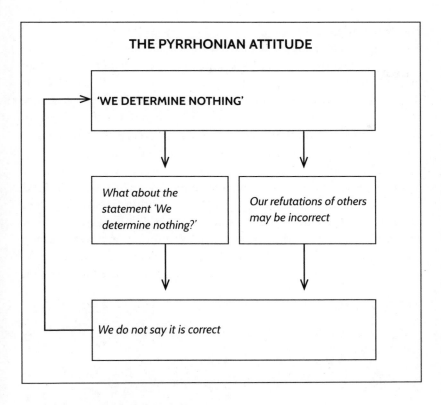

The Pyrrhonian school was extremely thorough and consistent in its denial of claims. Unsurprisingly they contested fiercely the assertions and claims of others, yet they did not excuse themselves from self-examination. On the contrary, Pyrrhonians claimed that they themselves asserted nothing; not even the refutation of the views they opposed. Instead they declared 'we determine nothing', leaving open the possibility that even their refutations of opponents were incorrect.

In practice the goal of this school was a suspension of judgement, in Greek *epoche*. So understood, this suspension of judgement was at least in part a coming to terms with our limitations of knowledge. Accepting these limitations leads to a type of peace, a philosophical tranquillity. Whether this was an aim of the philosophy or merely a fortuitous outcome, this tranquillity promised an escape from the disturbances of the world.

The Ten Modes

The Pyrrhonians adopted a method of ten modes or methods. The precise purpose of these modes is a matter of debate and it would be incorrect to claim that they form a type of system. Rather, it seems that they were used with the intention to generate doubt in the certainty of sense perceptions and thoughts, and by so doing either to refute dogmatic beliefs about these mental states, or at least lay the groundwork for alternative and seemingly mutually exclusive explanation.

The first mode points out that animals differ in their estimation of pleasure and goodness. For example, hemlock is fatal to men, but food for quail. The second mode states that, even within the same species, for example man, animals differ in their natures. For instance, one man enjoys playing cards, while another enjoys hunting and yet another, reading literature. The third mode concerns the differences in senses in a single animal. For example, the apple differs among itself to a person.

Hemlock is both poison to men and food for quail

For in taste it is sweet, in sight it is red, and in smell, odorous. In the fourth mode, we are reminded that, depending on our condition, whether it's being asleep, awake, in sickness, in old age, or in an emotional state, we experience things differently.

Conditions like sleep affect how we experience things

The fifth mode is that customs and laws differ between cultures, so that things as diverse as beauty, value and legality can change drastically from place to place. The sixth mode says that we cannot know how anything is in itself, for circumstances and conditions alter how it behaves and is perceived. A large rock is heavy only in air, for when put into water it can easily be moved about. The seventh mode refers to the relative position and placement of things and how this alters the perception of them. The sun, because of its great distance, appears small, while a straight line perceived at a certain angle appears crooked. Similarly, the eighth mode concerns the relative quantity or quality of things. Too little food leaves one hungry, enough gives satiety, while too much causes illness. The ninth mode concerns familiarity and unfamiliarity.

Earth tremors or falling snow are not unusual occurrences to those who constantly experience them. The tenth mode concerns relations of things. Thus the measure of strong and weak or of up and down depend on their relationship to something else and not upon some independent and objective fact about their nature. That is, 'up' is only up in relation to, for example, a pond and not to a tree, or strong is only strong in relation to, for example, a child and not to a weightlifter.

We may be strong, but only in comparison to a child and not a weightlifter

■ THE TEN MODES OF PYRRHONIAN SCEPTICISM

1. Differences among animals
2. Differences among humans
3. Differences of sense faculties
4. Differences of psychological condition
5. Differences of cultural relativism
6. Differences of circumstances and conditions
7. Differences of appearances
8. Differences of quantity and quality
9. Differences of acquaintance and novelty
10. Differences of relations

Key points

- A few generations after Plato's death, the Academy embraced scepticism under Arcesilaus who, on the basis of duplicates of things, such as twins, and on the illusory nature of dreams, doubted perception and advocated a suspension of belief.

- Carneades led the Academy after Arcesilaus and as a concession to daily living advocated a principle of the probable, whereby more important issues require a higher standard of probability and less important issues require a lower standard of probability.

- Carneades believed that cognitive impressions do not exist and that non-cognitive impressions are not to be indulged, thus leaving the only option as withholding belief.

- Pyrrho founded Pyrrhonian Scepticism, taking over from Academic Scepticism, and advocated complete suspension of belief or *epoche*, which when applied to others as equally as to themselves resulted in having no opinions about anything and a type of peace.

- The Pyrrhonians had ten modes intended to induce, justify or exemplify scepticism and cast doubt on dogmatic beliefs or, alternatively, create scepticism about belief in a general way.

Chapter 15

The Stoics

The Stoic philosophers were named after the location they frequented for their philosophical discussions and lectures, 'painted portico', *stoa poikile* in Greek, in the marketplace of Athens. Famous murals by Polygnotus and others lined the portico, yet

The Stoics got their name from their meetings in the stoa poikile *in Athens*

in the beginning the adherents of this sect were called Zenonians. This is because the founder of Stoicism was Zeno of Citium (*c.*333–262BC). The subsequent and equally influential heads of the school were Cleanthes (*c.*330–232BC) and Chrysippus (*c.*280–206BC).

The first work of Zeno, now lost, was entitled the *Republic*, the same Greek word Plato used for his influential book. A later philosopher summarized its contents as a depiction of men living without the associations of cities or tribes. Rather, all people lived as one, a cosmopolitan order arranged and maintained not by the proscriptions of a

Zeno of Citium was the founder of the Stoic movement

parochial interest, but the universal dictates of reason. This conception of Zeno's philosophical work serves as a good starting point for the elaboration of the rest of his system, for due to the loss of his works, we must be content with deriving his guiding principles from the work of his successors.

Ethics

The Stoics divided philosophy into ethics, physics and logic, a classification influential before and after the zenith of their own system. As to ethics, their single, overriding and often controversial thesis was that virtue alone was sufficient for happiness. Good, in the realm of moral progress, was consequently dependent and defined only in terms of the possession of virtue. This notion of the good, and along with it the pursuit of happiness, excluded from it the accumulation of possessions, money, fame, sex, and even health. This is not to say that there were

Arête, or virtue, was the ultimate aspiration for most philosophers of the time

prohibitions on their possession. Rather, it is to affirm that virtue alone was sufficient for the good life and for happiness.

It is important to remember that virtue, *arête* in Greek, was for the Stoics, as well as for the general philosophical community of the time, a term which denoted excellence when held in both the moral and intellectual spheres. As a necessary result, since virtue was the only good, no things were bad provided only that virtue was achieved and retained. This is to say that conventional things like death or disease were not considered bad because they could potentially lead to the possession of virtue and, more importantly, they had no necessary connection to the possession of virtue. The great number of things which are considered good by the common run of people, such as money or fame, were termed 'indifferent', *adiaphora* in Greek, by the Stoics, denoting that their possession was indifferent to the status of virtue, but not that they were disvalued completely or that they retarded moral growth. These indifferent goods, just like the indifferent bad things, attained their worth by relation to each other, but not in relation to virtue. Whatever the Stoic self-characterization of the virtuous life, a great deal of their moral system depends on the mental outlook which they applied to the 'goods', 'bads' and 'indifferents' of the world.

In Accordance with Nature

The Stoic moral system always sought to align itself with virtue and, at a greater scale, to live this life in accordance with nature. The best way to understand this is to understand that the moral landscape for Stoics was embedded within the entire universe. Man was just one part of this living organism of the cosmos and if his role was rendered ineffectual or corrupted in some way, then to this degree the state of the world was harmed.

The impulse to align action with nature is closely related to another Stoic concept. This unique doctrine was called *oikeiosis*. Literally it is derived from 'that which is one's own' in contrast to *allotrion*, that which is foreign. The term 'affinity' seems to be the best single-word translation into English. In affinity, we may imagine that when an animal first comes into the world it feels an immediate attachment to its own life and existence. Thus it pursues those things that contribute to its own

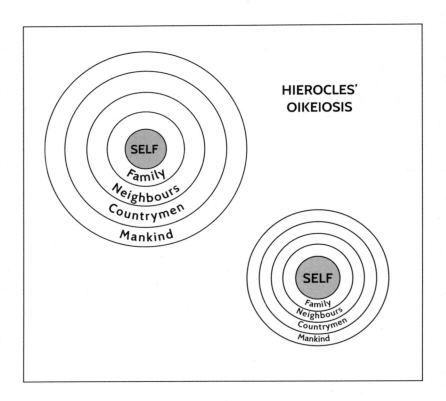

HIEROCLES'
OIKEIOSIS

SELF
Family
Neighbours
Countrymen
Mankind

SELF
Family
Neighbours
Countrymen
Mankind

survival, development, and current and future wellbeing. This feeling, to put it another way, amounts to the fact that it would be unnatural for an animal to be alienated from itself, ignoring the instinct to care for the progress of its own life. This affinity is not limited to animals, but applies to all of creation.

In the case of man, affinity undergoes a rather sophisticated development when, at the appropriate age, he acquires the faculty and the use of reason. This natural change awakens in him an impulse toward the ethical life, including no longer only pursuing his own interests, but enlarging them to include the family and his city. As an illustration of the idea that affinity itself matures and grows, Hierocles, a later Stoic, imagined a series of circles concentrically enclosing groups of people. At the centre is the self, but in the larger circles going outward, the family, neighbours, and countrymen each envelop the previous circle until finally the last encompasses mankind as a whole, and the furthest circle is cinched inwards so that one treats any member of mankind like his brother.

Moral Choices

The moral distinctions deployed by the Stoics are in three main categories. The first category is that which is morally 'choice-worthy', those actions which ought to be pursued. The second category is bad things or actions that ought to be rejected or 'to be repudiated'. The third and last category is actions that are neither good nor bad, but are 'indifferent'. Although indifferent, these actions could be further classified as 'preferred indifferent' or 'dispreferred indifferent'. The determinative qualification for a preferred indifferent was whether choosing that option would contribute to a morally good life. Because these qualifications were situated in the midst of a moral vocabulary aiming for a good life, the categories themselves came to be described by their utility. The morally good was 'useful' and 'helpful', the bad was 'harmful', while the indifferents were either 'advantageous' or 'disadvantageous'. Of course the recognition and the pursuit of all these variables in real life required the cultivation of a practical wisdom.

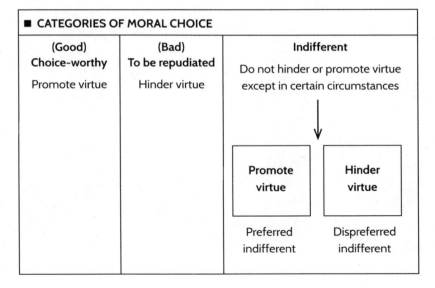

■ CATEGORIES OF MORAL CHOICE

(Good) Choice-worthy	(Bad) To be repudiated	Indifferent
Promote virtue	Hinder virtue	Do not hinder or promote virtue except in certain circumstances

	Promote virtue	Hinder virtue
	Preferred indifferent	Dispreferred indifferent

Stoic Sage

In the ideal of the sage, the Stoics conceived of a person who was suited to sift through the day-to-day choices with the wisdom afforded him by right reason. That is, he does everything well because he is a master at the art of life. As such, some later Stoics conceded that such a philosopher does not, or rarely, exists. Nevertheless, this is the ideal towards which all may hope to attain, with one who is making progress toward such a goal called 'one making progress', *prokopton* in Greek. The current use of the

The sage was to avoid the four passions of fear, lust, pain and pleasure

word 'Stoic', meaning without emotion, is somewhat accurate to the old philosophy. The Stoics believed that excessive passions, four in number – fear, lust, pain, pleasure – were disobedient to reason, and thus to be avoided by the practised sage.

Physics

The Stoics believed in the common substances discussed in Greek physics: earth, air, water and fire. Ultimately, though, matter and God were behind these four elements. Air and fire were the active elements, evidenced by their motion, while earth and water were passive.

God is the active and matter is the passive principle, the former working on the latter in the sense of shaping the matter. In this way God is considered the *logos*, a Greek word loaded with linguistic depth: word, meaning, definition, logic, formula. When something possessed life, it had a mixture of the active air and fire. As such, the soul, *psyche* in Greek, was a material entity, not a ghostly, ephemeral wisp as in popular imagination. This soul stretches through the body, wherein its centre, near the heart, is the *hegemonikon*, the leading part of the soul, the centre of reason.

STOIC PHYSICAL THEORY

Air	Active	God as 'logos'	Active
Fire			
Water	Passive	Matter	Passive
Earth			

One of the more incredible and memorable parts of Stoic physics is the belief in the repetition of the world order in all its detail, after the world itself ends in a cosmic conflagration. Only a residue of the previous reality would remain from this fire, after which, a new world order arises.

Logic

Stoics were well regarded for their work on logic, which included not only what we consider formal logic, but also dialectic, rhetoric, grammar and language more generally. One area of interest was their attention on sayables or speakables, *lekta* in Greek. This refers to the meaning but not the sound or written letters of a word. The Stoics recognized that these speakables were not physical things and assigned to them a kind of secondary level of existence. As a result, to the delight of their critics, the meanings of words paradoxically could not be a cause of things, because causes had to be physical. When sayables are combined into a sentence form that can be evaluated as to whether they are true or not, they are called assertibles. In addition to these linguistic categories, Stoics studied and developed the form of the logical syllogism, which is composed out of assertibles.

Lastly, the Stoic theory of knowledge involved the assent of the mind only to true impressions. Cicero, the Latin writer, captured this in an anecdote about Zeno. An open hand is like an impression, the closed hand is as an assent to the impression, while the fist, tightly clenched, is comprehension, *katalepsis* in Greek (literally 'grasping'), of the original impression.

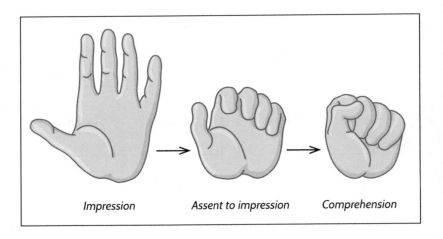

Impression   Assent to impression   Comprehension

Key points

- Stoics divided philosophy into ethics, physics and logic.

- The moral system of the Stoics gave value only to the possession of virtue, relegating all other so-called goods to a morally indifferent status.

- A virtuous life was considered a life in accordance with nature, which in the case of mankind meant in accordance with right reason.

- *Oikeiosis* or affinity was an idea that we are born with an innate tendency for self-care, but as part of a universe, our right reason should lead us to enlarge this concern outwards from ourselves to all of mankind.

- Stoics divided actions into choice-worthy, worthy of repudiation, or indifferent, the latter being either preferred or dispreferred, depending only on whether the indifferent action would lead to a morally good life.

- Although the Stoics accepted the four common Greek elements, they believed that God, the active principle, and matter, the passive principle, were the most fundamental explanations of the world.

Chapter 16

Epicurus

The Garden

Epicurus (*c.*341–270BC) was born in Athens, illustrious home of many Greek philosophers, but raised on the island of Samos, a new colony from the mother city. He reportedly was a teacher of grammar, but then later was drawn to philosophy after reading the work of Democritus. His zeal was such that he was able to convert his three brothers to the study of philosophy as well. At a later time, he returned to Athens for the institution of a 'Garden', in which his philosophical disciples and brethren could reside and flourish among a dedicated community. Eventually the Epicureans became associated with this location, and the Garden came to refer to the Epicurean school.

Epicurus was a grammar teacher who turned to philosophy after reading the works of Democritus

Epicurus created a 'Garden' in Athens for philosophers to debate and discuss their ideas

The *Tetrapharmakon*

Epicurus' *Principal Doctrines*, a work entirely written in a series of dogmatic and conclusive aphorisms, begins with four ideas, upheld by later Epicureans as the epitome of their lived philosophy. They called this grouping the 'four-fold remedy', *tetrapharmakon* in Greek. This four-fold remedy is a clear and accurate representation of the foundation of the Epicurean ethical system. The first doctrine is that the 'blessed and immortal' neither gives nor receives trouble. The gods, that is, are aloof from the world; they do not interfere in the affairs of the world and certainly do not prepare an afterlife of punishment or pleasure for mortals. As such, the second doctrine follows, that 'death is nothing to us'.

According to the Epicureans, the gods stayed aloof from the mortal world and it was a mistake to live one's life in preparation for the afterlife

The double meaning this sentence conveys for us in English is the same in Greek. Death is both a thing of no worth to us and, since sensation is that which characterizes life while death is without sensation, death is not a thing we can experience. The third doctrine was the topic of pleasure. Epicurus' advice here is that there is a limit as to the degree of pleasure. This limit is not how much food can be devoured nor sex indulged, but simply the removal of that which is painful. Corresponding to this advice on pleasure is the fourth doctrine, concerning the limits of pain. Pain is of two types, chronic and acute. We may take solace that acute pain lasts a short time, while chronic pain still allows for the predominance of pleasure over pain. In summary then, the divine nature and death are no concern of ours, while pleasure and pain must be understood as limited in their respective ways.

■ FOUR-FOLD REMEDY (*Tetrapharmakon*)	
1 The gods cannot be troubled and do not trouble us. 2 Death is nothing to us for we are not there to experience it.	Out of our control, unknown to us
3 The limit of pleasure is removal of pain. 4 Pain is limited in either degree or duration.	In our control, known to us

When these teachings are grasped and applied properly, then life may be led with pleasure and blessedness. The summary of these teachings may be best encapsulated in a peculiarly Epicurean word, *ataraxia*, a freedom from pain and want.

Physics

In the Epicurean system with its privileged cultivation of pleasure, it can be difficult to understand the emphasis Epicurus places on the physical makeup of the universe. In one of the sayings from *Principal Doctrines*, he clarifies the relationship in this way: 'It would not be possible to dissolve the object of fear unless someone knows what is the nature of the universe.' If we are ignorant of some feature of the universe, then this could play upon and play into our fear, such as a threat or the gods' vengeance.

We learn of Epicurus' physics chiefly through the *Letter to Pythocles* and the *Letter to Herodotus*. At the outset he makes clear that the degree of certainty for things which occur in the cosmos, as opposed to directly on the earth, are more difficult to ascertain. We should approach this kind of study with less certainty, therefore, and be willing to give more than one explanation to fit the phenomenon. Our guide is to form an analogy, as best we can, from earthly phenomena to heavenly phenomena. A good example of this sort of explanation is lightning, which has three possible causes: either it is caused by the release of fire atoms, or by external fire atoms, or by wind. Each explanation also has multiple ways it could be realized.

Lightning could be explained by three causes – the release of fire atoms, external fire atoms, or the wind

Epicurus considered worlds to be infinite, meaning there are countless other solar systems, of course with a planet at the centre of each. His explanation of the multitude of worlds fits squarely into his programme of origins, for he also discusses the formation of clouds, rain, thunder and lightning. In the course of these descriptions and explanations we remedy our own ignorance, shielding it from fear, but we also come to learn that the workings of the universe are not wound by the clockwork interference of divine activity.

Atomism

With naturalistic, non-divine explanation in the background, Epicurus directs us to his atomism, a belief that everything is composed of countless and indestructible atoms in continuous motion. These atoms have always existed and will continue on into the endless future. Atoms have a weight compelling them downwards towards the bottom of the universe to which they are always descending.

In the midst of this descent, there is a notorious account of the occasional action of the atoms. There is sometimes a 'swerve' wherein the normal linear descent of atoms, in parallel, is disrupted. There are at least two significant consequences of this theory. The first is that the atoms which compose the secondary bodies, that is, the bodies which are composed from and so dependent on atoms, must at some point have deviated from their strict path, or else the secondary bodies would never have come to be. The second consequence is that this slight deviation of the atoms gives a philosophical justification to the existence of free will, otherwise inexplicable by atomism. Without the swerve there would be no free will, everything would follow as the strict result of atoms predictably and necessarily falling straight through the depths of the universe.

In addition to atoms, there is the void, understood best as that which is the space in which atoms can move. Thus, a void is posited for the possibility of motion. It is within this void that atoms fall. These two elements, void and material atoms, make up the nature of the universe. The universe is infinite in extent and the number of atoms, while there is also an infinity of worlds.

Epicurus' atomism is all-encompassing, so that even the soul is material, a fact which Epicurus regards as of deep importance, for it sets the terms of our reality, a mortal toil which is composed from and will decompose back into some group of atoms. The mind is likewise atomic, since a material existence enables the mind to be able to interact with the physical body. The only other possibility in the universe beside physical matter is void, Epicurus points out. Yet it would be impossible if the soul were made out of void, for then it could not act nor be acted upon, for the void is nothing.

Logic

Epicurus' logic, or theory of knowledge, was based upon the *Canonic*, a work that has not survived. Nevertheless, we have enough of his philosophy from others to claim a fair intimacy with his conception of knowledge. Our sense perception is the foundation of our knowledge, a guarantee of its truthfulness. Thus, the sense perceptions, along with preconceptions and feelings, are the three sources of knowledge.

The authenticity and reliability of sense perception owes to the elementary nature of its production: the sense organs simply report what is out there in the world, a mechanical fidelity ultimately traceable to an utterly material universe.

A preconception is an idea gathered from many occasions. For example, a continual exposure to dogs forms a preconception of the idea of a dog, which we could then use to understand other instances

SOURCES OF KNOWLEDGE

	Sense Perception	Preconception	Feeling (Pleasure or Pain)
Example	Seeing a dog	Idea of a dog	Being bitten by a dog
Dependence on matter	Images are sent from dog to eye	Dependent on seeing many dogs	Pain is the disruption of atoms

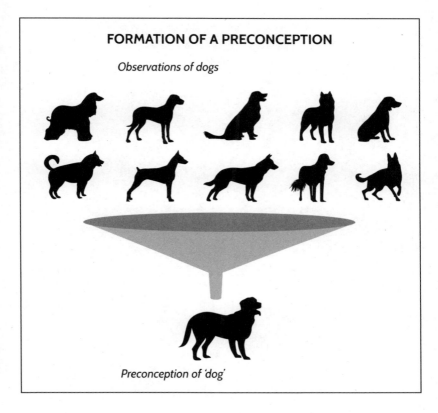

FORMATION OF A PRECONCEPTION

Observations of dogs

Preconception of 'dog'

of dog. Just as with sense perception, a preconception is dependent on perception as well, and for this reason is considered to be just as reliable.

Feelings are divided into pleasure and pain, the two principles used by humans in determining courses of choice or avoidance. The reliability of pleasure and pain as criteria of truth comes from the indubitability of the feelings themselves. You may be mistaken in thinking you are smart, or that you have turned off the oven, when you have not, but it is impossible that you could be mistaken in the experience of personal pain or pleasure.

Vision is an intriguing example of Epicurean sense perception. Epicurus believed that a stream of images emanates from objects and is carried to our eyes. Because the images resemble their objects in position and order, a faithful representation of the object is perceived. His technical

Epicurus claimed that the sun was exactly the size it appeared to be, only to be ridiculed by his fellow philosophers for this assertion

term for such images was *eidola*. Now, although he allowed that there could be deception in vision, Epicurus denied that the falsity owed to the perception itself. Instead, he insisted that misperception or illusion arises when we add our own opinion to the perception, distorting the fidelity of the *eidola*. One obstinate result of this conviction is that Epicurus insisted that the size of the sun was exactly as large as it appeared, an assertion that garnered a fair bit of mockery.

Aristippus was one of the leading Cyrenaics, a rival group to the Epicureans who placed the pleasure of the body above everything else

The Cyrenaics believed that only bodily pleasure was to be pursued

Pleasure

We return to and end with pleasure because of its centrality to the Epicurean philosophical life. Pleasure is 'the beginning and the end of the living blessedly' and if this were not praise enough, 'the first and innate good' for us. A later rival group to the Epicureans, the Cyrenaics, held that only bodily pleasure was to be pursued. Yet the standard Epicurean belief was that not every pleasure is to be chosen, but only those (at the opportune time) that are conducive to living well, with both advantage and disadvantage weighed. Therefore the cultivation of this kind of prudence is not only sufficient for happiness, but it also stands at the head of other virtues, for in knowing the limits of pleasure and pain, it also tells of the path to happiness.

Key points

- Epicurus' four-fold remedy or *tetrapharmakon* sums up his ethics – the first and second remedies, the gods and death, are out of our control and unknown to us, and the third and fourth remedies, pleasure and pain, are in our control and known to us.

- In the four-fold remedy: first, the gods are removed and indifferent to things which occur in our mortal world; second, death cannot be known and therefore is nothing to us; third, there is a limit to pleasure, the removal of all pain; fourth, there are two types of pain: acute pains that do not last long and chronic pains that allow the possibility of more bodily pleasure than pain.

- Epicurus proposed that the universe is made out of atoms and void, and as atoms fall downward into the void, unpredictably a swerve in one of the atoms comes about, which accounts for free will and the combination of atoms into larger secondary bodies.

- Epicurus' three sources of knowledge are sense perception, preconceptions and feelings.

- The sense organs simply report what is out there in the world, in vision, for example, images or *eidola* stream off objects, faithfully representing to the observer the thing being seen; a preconception arises when we see many instances and form an idea from the instances; and feelings can be resolved into pain and pleasure, each of which is indubitable.

- The pursuit of pleasure was the life of happiness for Epicurus, but this involves a wisdom that takes into account all the advantages and disadvantages attending choosing a given pleasure.

Chapter 17

Lucretius

ON THE NATURE OF THINGS

Lucretius (99–55BC), revered for his literary as well as philosophical influence, was a Roman poet and philosopher, an artistic evangelist for the cause of Epicurus and his doctrines. We know very little about the man himself. The only anecdote we have from antiquity is that Lucretius was driven mad from a love potion, wrote his poem *De Rerum Natura* and committed suicide. He was born within several years of both Julius Caesar and Cicero, the later of whom was said to have edited and proofread Lucretius' work after his death.

The only surviving work of Lucretius is *De Rerum Natura*. This is often referred to by its Latin title, and translates as *On the Nature of Things*, *How Things Are*, or *The Nature of the Universe*; the word 'things' in this context often meant reality as a whole. Lucretius composed this work in Latin dactylic hexameter; the same meter used by the Greek epic poets, and perhaps more importantly by the philosophers Empedocles and Parmenides. Just as the intent of those philosophers was to teach their philosophy through the medium of poetry, Lucretius aimed at the spread of his message. At one point he draws a parallel between those who sweeten the brim of a cup of bitter medicine with honey and his own work of putting Epicurus into poetic form.

The Poem's Dedication

The heart of the poem is strictly Epicurean, but this does not mean that Lucretius did not add his own artistic flourish nor consolidate the underlying philosophy with force or subtlety, as appropriate. The poem has a broad ambition to convert many to the philosophy of Epicurus, but it is dedicated to the hopeful conversion of Gaius Memmius, a notable Roman politician. Breaking new literary ground as the first to

Lucretius was a Roman philosopher and follower of Epicurus

put a systematic philosophy into verse, Lucretius repeatedly laments the inability of Latin to fully articulate the abstract concepts birthed in the Greek tongue. An additional element of the poem, in contrast to Epicurus, is the polemical aim Lucretius takes at the doctrines of secret Presocratics – Plato, Aristotle and the Stoics – frequently without directly naming his opponent.

The Structure of the Poem

Lucretius' philosophical poem was written in six books. The six books are thematically paired, with Books 1 and 2 explicating the doctrines of atomism, Books 3 and 4, the mortal material of the mind and soul, while Books 5 and 6 are concerned with the makeup and dissolution of the world, as well as an explanation of its phenomena.

STRUCTURE OF *DE RERUM NATURA*

Book 1	Atoms and Void	Atomic Theory
Book 2	Properties and movements of Atoms	
Book 3	Mortality of mind and soul	Psychological Theory
Book 4	Perception and thought	
Book 5	Genesis and formation of the world	Natural Explanations
Book 6	Various phenomena, disease, death and plague	

Strangely, Lucretius began his great philosophical work with a tribute to the goddess Venus

Book 1

Oddly, for a proponent of divine indifference, Lucretius begins his poem with an extended invocation of the goddess Venus. So peculiar is its placement here, that either Lucretius himself or a subsequent editor has inserted a section from later on in the poem directly after this address to the goddess. In the insertion, Lucretius asserts the unmolested peace the gods enjoy. Along with Venus, Lucretius also praises Epicurus as the bringer of liberating knowledge. Notorious as a philosophical patron of atheism, Epicurus is instead praised as the vanquisher of religion and superstition, which is the true instigator of outrageous, wicked deeds. Religion to the Epicurean eye was nothing more than a source of fear of the afterlife and wicked actions masked under the name of piety.

In the rest of Book 1 Lucretius sets forth atomism and attacks rival material theories. Faithful to Epicurus, Lucretius emphasizes the reality of atoms and the void, as well as the detailed nature and behaviour of atoms, explaining the existence of all else as dependent on atoms and void. One famously ingenious argument for the infinitude of the

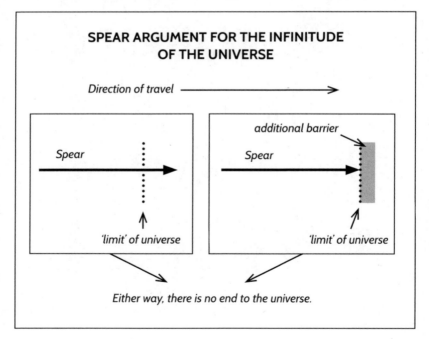

SPEAR ARGUMENT FOR THE INFINITUDE OF THE UNIVERSE

Direction of travel ⟶

Spear

'limit' of universe

additional barrier

Spear

'limit' of universe

Either way, there is no end to the universe.

universe involves a spear and an Epicurean imagination. We are to envision approaching the edge of the universe with a spear in hand, then letting it go. There are only two possibilities, either the spear continues past the edge of the universe or something stops it after it has passed the edge. The first scenario, wherein the spear sails past the universe's boundary is clearly a proof that there really is no boundary, because the area 'past the boundary of existence' clearly exists as well. The second option may seem more promising to someone who denies the universe is infinite. However, the fact that the spear is impeded after it has crossed the limit of the universe shows that there is something past the limit, namely this wall or obstruction and the place it takes up. Therefore, concludes Lucretius, whether the spear hits something or not, there can be no end of the universe.

Book 2

Beginning with delight in the possession of Epicurean knowledge, Lucretius then shifts to a description of atomic motion, followed by their shape, size and weight beyond which they possess no other distinguishing qualities. The atoms are themselves in perpetual motion and fall at astonishing speeds because they are not impeded by anything in the void. Despite the variety of atomic weights, the heavier atoms do not outstrip the lighter ones, Lucretius says, because the void gives no resistance to all the atoms equally.

Epicurus' swerve, a doctrine that allows for the possibility of free will, is given a more precise treatment here. Atoms would fall straight down, like rain from the sky, if there were no swerve. But the swerve is as random as it is slight; it is no more than an imperceptible deviation. The swerve must occur, Lucretius hypothesises, at this extremely minimal level to account for both the fact that things always seem to fall perfectly straight and as a condition for free will, which could not exist in a material world completely determined by atoms predictably falling straight down.

Book 3

There are two elements we may call the soul, *anima* in Latin, and the mind, *animus* in Latin, in our bodies, but we must acknowledge that they

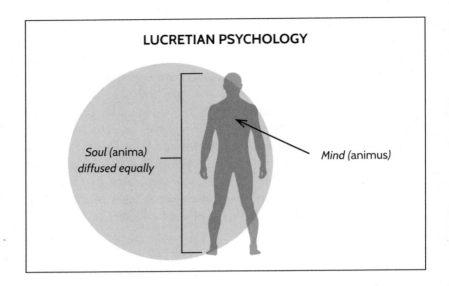

too are material. While the mind is the command centre, the soul is more of a life force. The soul is dispersed throughout the body, but the mind is located in the chest.

The atoms of the mind and soul are extremely small, smooth and round. This allows the mind to move quickly and nimbly, and the soul to permeate the body.

Lucretius embarks on an ambitious attack on the immortality of soul and mind. One argument makes a mockery of an immortal soul leaving the body to fly heavenwards. If souls fly heavenward at death, he argues, then it would mean the air were alive, for it would possess a soul. Against a belief in reincarnation where people become animals or vice versa, Lucretius raises the point that this does not fit with the fact that different animals have consistent traits, such as foxes being clever or the timidity of deer.

Lucretius ends by proposing some arguments against the fear of death. In the 'Symmetry argument' he makes the point that just as we did not, nor do we now, lament or worry about ourselves before we came to exist, so too why should we worry about our state after death? We did not exist before we were born nor will we exist after we are dead, so who exactly will suffer the harm of death? He also likens life to a banquet,

SYMMETRY ARGUMENT AGAINST FEAR OF DEATH

Before Birth	Our Life	Death
Time before our existence	Time of our existence	Time after death
No concern of ours	Our concern	No concern of ours

after which a guest peacefully retires into the night. We too gladly accede to death, after we have had our fill of life.

Book 4

Book 4 endorses the Epicurean view of the senses, echoing many of Epicurus' explanations of perception, especially the nature of vision as a reception of images, while other sensations are also explained in a material manner. Importantly, Lucretius denies that any parts of our bodies were 'made to see' or 'made to think'. This owes both to the explanatory power of atomism on its own, but also because it would involve the gods' interference in the creation of our world, an intervention that would disturb their blessed peace.

Book 5

Book 5 tells that the nature of our world is such that it will eventually be annihilated, but for now the earth is at the middle of the world. Lucretius also addresses various cosmological phenomena, such as the orbits of different bodies, phases of the moon, eclipses and the length of daytime.

In a striking image of naturalist zoology, Lucretius describes the creation of plants and animals at the beginning of our planet. They were

In an echo of modern evolutionary theory, the first humans only emerged after the ill-formed plants and animals of the planet's early years had died off

awkwardly formed and ill-suited to live, thus they died from this biological misfortune. After a time, primitive humans emerged. Lucretius engages in an elaborate history of the cultural growth of humanity, beginning with language and ending with the cultivation of the arts.

Book 6

Much as the beginning of *De Rerum Natura* has puzzled commentators, so has the finish of Book 6, which ends in death, disease and plague. Mostly it continues on from the previous book, offering natural explanations of puzzling phenomena such as the consistent water level of the ocean or the origin of clouds. However, the last few hundred lines broach the topic of disease. Here Lucretius says that noxious particles suffuse the air and cause disease to those who breathe it, and citing other climates, points out how much their weather varies. At the very end, Lucretius describes the terrible plague which once afflicted Athens, going into graphic detail about black stools, puss-filled blood, and the desperate severing of genitals to alleviate suffering.

Key points

- *On the Nature of Things* or *De Rerum Natura* is the title of Lucretius' only surviving work, composed after both literary and philosophical models and divided into six books.

- Faithful to Epicurus' philosophy, Book 1 concerns the atoms and the void, and the notion that the universe is infinite, and Book 2 lays out the details of atomic behaviour, including an explanation of the swerve and free will.

- Book 3 concerns the mind and the soul. Both are mortal and material, the soul permeates the body and the mind is located in the chest; arguments against the immortality of the soul include the Symmetry argument and the Banquet argument.

- Book 4 looks at the material nature of sense perception, especially the nature of vision as a reception of images, again rejecting divine design.

- Book 5 involves a history of the world, including human society, with an insistence on its eventual destruction, and a precursor of biological natural selection, and Book 6 culminates with death, disease and a plague that beset Athens.

Chapter 18

Seneca

Seneca (1BC–65AD) was a Stoic philosopher, poet and statesman writing in Latin in the first century. He was born into wealth and pursued the expected political life of a man of his rank. One of several interesting facts of this man's life was that he was convicted and sentenced to death for adultery with the wife of Gaius Caesar. History has largely viewed the conviction with suspicion; indeed, the emperor Claudius reduced the sentence to mere exile, often taken as an acknowledgement of a dubious conviction. It was when he was recalled from exile that he became the personal tutor to the infamous emperor Nero, who at a later date requested the philosopher to cut his wrists, little more than a forced suicide, in one of

Seneca was both a statesman and a philosopher who became the tutor to the infamous emperor Nero

the enduring images of courage from antiquity. Seneca wrote in many genres including tragedy and epistle, and even within philosophy itself he wrote diversely on moral questions concerning the natural world and empathetic consolations for those he loved.

An Eclectic Stoicism

Later writers have often criticized Seneca for being eclectic or compromising in his Stoicism, but he insisted that he was orthodox and committed to the advancement of his school. In addition, although

Seneca wrote several works and paid much attention to the philosophers that came before him, including Plato, Aristotle, Epicurus and the many Stoics that inspired him having interests in the physics and logic of Stoicism, it was primarily living well and the virtuous life which captured his philosophical attention. To what degree he was fully Stoic is difficult to determine, but he was certainly not a systematic or narrowly sectarian philosopher. Thus he engages with a great variety of philosophical material, including Plato, Aristotle, Epicureanism and of course fellow Stoics. For this reason, a comprehensive reading or depiction of his philosophy is nearly impossible. He consciously wrote philosophical Latin, an oddity, for even the Roman emperor Marcus Aurelius, who was also a Stoic, wrote in Greek, the traditional language of the Greek *stoa*.

Moral Epistles

Seneca's collection *Moral Epistles* is often considered his most influential and developed work. In it, he addresses a series of letters to Lucilius, his friend of the equestrian order. As could be supposed for a Stoic work, the focus of the epistles is a preoccupation with the centrality of virtue. These letters cover material in such a way as to encourage a morally Stoic way of life as one 'making progress', *proficiens* in Latin, toward the ideal. In somewhat of a paradox, Seneca laid great emphasis on the will, encouraging the acceptance of the providence of nature, prodding

Crowds at executions had a corrupting influence according to Seneca

a submission of the role of our will in pursuing the virtues of the soul. It is clear that he has philosophical forebears in mind when writing these letters, for he promises fame to Lucilius, just as Epicurus gave to Idomeneus, and Cicero gave to Atticus.

The topics he discusses in these letters, sometimes brief, sometimes spanning several pages, involve, among other things, how to spend one's time, the avoidance of the fear of death, and the maliciousness and corrupting influence of crowds at executions. There is often an overlapping of themes or specific topics elsewhere in his corpus, such as in his works *On Leisure* and *On the Tranquillity of the Mind*.

On Benefits

On Benefits is a work of seven books in which Seneca focuses on the proper distribution and reception of benefits or favours. This highly practical work discusses the moral value of the act of giving: one must acknowledge the gift one has received in the form of a favour.

Can a child do greater favours for their parents than they received from them?

In fact, ingratitude is among the worst kinds of human evils, its most pernicious form being forgetfulness. Along with the imperative of repaying favours, Seneca offers advice on how, with what attitude, and with what speed to give favours, and whether to give favours secretly or openly.

He also deals with some specifically Roman questions on benefits. He addresses whether a slave can do favours for his master (yes), and whether children can do greater favours for their parents than their parents did for them (yes). Seneca sees a distinction between the activity of the favour, *beneficium* in Latin, and the substance of that favour, *materia beneficii* in Latin.

■ PARTS OF FAVOUR OR BENEFIT	
Activity *(beneficium)*	**Substance** *(materia beneficii)*

It is actually the activity of the favour which for Seneca carries the moral force of the gift. Under this framework it is really only the mind and attitude which has any moral value. Accordingly, a gift, at least in its concrete expression, is merely a sign of the underlying reality of the actual benefit.

On Anger

On Anger is another venture into practical philosophy, with the aim of answering Novatus' question about how to minimize the power of anger. Seneca characterizes it as a brute and the fiercest, least human of the passions. He addresses the view that anger can be put to good use, disagreeing entirely, denigrating the passion as something wholly against nature. Anger itself, he says, is in response to a perceived wrong. There is first an involuntary impulse, *adfectus* in Latin, which is a result of this impression. At the next step the mind is free to assent or not to this impulse. When it does, then there results a bold striking out with the goal of revenge, *poena* in Latin.

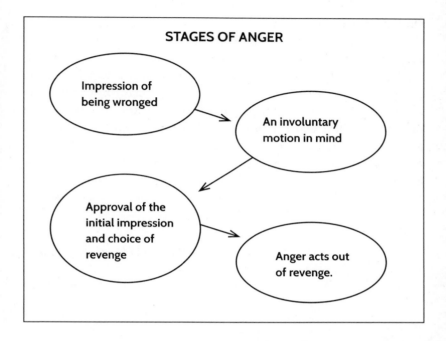

STAGES OF ANGER

Impression of being wronged

An involuntary motion in mind

Approval of the initial impression and choice of revenge

Anger acts out of revenge.

Children must be educated in the process of anger, so that they do not give in to its allure as adults. Adults, on the other hand, have to develop the discipline of never succumbing to the siren call of anger's first impulse. Finally, even if these preventatives fail, one must appeal to right reason and fight, even against oneself, to quell the onset of anger.

On Providence

Despite the title of *On Providence*, not attested in Seneca's time, the focus of this work is not on divine providence in the abstract, but as it applies to the life of good people. More specifically, it concerns the theological problem that has long plagued believers in divinity, namely, how can bad things happen to good people when a good god is provident over the world? Seneca's answer is to affirm the goodness and beneficence of the gods, to argue that the souls of those who are undergoing suffering are strengthened, moreover that this adversity benefits both them and society at large, and lastly that virtuous people cannot be wretched, because virtue alone is sufficient for happiness.

On the Happy Life

Of the utmost importance to living is how to live happily. Roughly divided into two parts, *On the Happy Life* first describes what the happy or blessed life consists of, and then proceeds to explain how this life can be achieved. Seneca toes the official Stoic line, emphasizing that living in accordance with nature is the path to a happy life. Reason is everywhere present in nature, and it is reason by which our own lives should be guided. In a surprising move on the topic of wealth, Seneca seems to admit that money can brighten the day of the wise man. Nevertheless, life must at all times be acknowledged as depending on the pursuit of virtue, choosing virtue at the expense of all other available choices.

Unlike most philosophers of the time, Seneca conceded that wealth was to be desired even by the wisest of men

On the Constancy of the Wise Man

In *On the Constancy of the Wise Man* Seneca confronts the Stoic paradox that the wise man, the ideal sage, cannot suffer harm or injury. This paradox is in fact an objection to the very way of life for Stoics. If virtue is not sufficient for life then Stoicism is philosophically vacuous. How can the sage be impervious to the searing metal of a branding iron shoved into his unsuspecting ribcage, for example? He distinguishes between two types of harm: 'slight', *contumelia* in Latin, and 'injury', *iniuria* in Latin. Injury is subject to legal redress, he claims, while slight is not. There is in this distinction a degree of qualitative difference; whereas the wise man is indeed subject to the experience of injury, he overcomes it, yet he does not even feel slights.

On Mercy

The disturbing irony of *On Mercy* is its dedication to the cruel and unjust emperor Nero. The political setting for the work makes it intriguing to those with an interest in imperial Roman power. In the setup for this work, Seneca addresses those who are already in power in addition to making the case that mercy, *clementia* in Latin, is a Roman virtue. Not only is it a virtue, but Seneca portrays mercy as a type of guiding principle for the ruler, for whom all other virtues are secondary. In this regard, the text has sometimes critically been viewed as an apology for tyranny.

In an ironic twist, Seneca's On Mercy was dedicated to one of the cruellest and most tyrannical rulers of ancient Rome, the emperor Nero

There is an uneasy slippage in the latter part of the work from monarch to the wise man, which further complicates the analysis of this text.

Consolations

Seneca wrote three consolations as solace and to encourage individuals in specific situations. In *Consolation to Marcia* Seneca addresses Marcia, who lost her son a few years before. He chides her for the indulgence of excess crying and contrasts selfish with unselfish mourning. In addition, he praises examples of those who have mourned correctly, while also providing precepts to follow. With much the same programme, his *Consolation to Polybius* is written to a freed slave whose brother has died. In the *Consolation to Helvia*, Seneca addresses his own mother, grieved over his very own exile. First, with the expected overtones of Stoic resolve, firmly committed to the idea that only virtue matters, Seneca assures his mother she need not mourn for him. He then points out to her that her own condition has nothing to be mourned.

Key points

- Seneca was a Roman Stoic writing in Latin, engaging in agreement and disagreement with other philosophical schools, and whose breadth and depth defied systemization.

- Seneca's most influential work is considered *The Moral Epistles*, a collection of letters encouraging a morally Stoic way of life, focusing on the centrality of virtue and emphasizing the role of the will in pursuing these virtues.

- *On Benefits*, Seneca's work of seven books, covers the distribution and reception of benefits or favours, and distinguishes between the activity of the favour and the substance of that favour, the former carrying the moral force of the gift.

- Seneca's Dialogues include: *On Anger*, offering a guide on rejecting what he called the anger impulse; *On Providence*, tackling the problem of evil; *On the Happy Life*, an exhortation to live in accordance with nature by right reason in pursuit of virtue; *On the Constancy of the Wise Man*, seeking to uphold the Stoic idea that the sage cannot be harmed; and *On Mercy*, arguing that mercy is a fundamentally Roman virtue and that for the ruler to whom it properly belongs, it is the chief virtue.

- Seneca's three consolations use previous exemplars of mourning and courage to exhort his addressee, as well as warning against excess, while couching this advice amidst an emphasis on the centrality of virtue.

Chapter 19

Epictetus

Epictetus was formerly a slave to a prominent member of Nero's court in Rome, though he wrote his philosophy in the *koine* Greek common to the time, a form of Greek also recorded in the New Testament. His writings are the *Discourses* and the *Enchiridion*, which is Greek for 'little handbook'. The *Handbook* was a distillation of the teachings of the former, while the *Discourses*, rather than having been written by Epictetus, were said to have been composed by Arrian, a student, as a faithful representation

Epictetus was both slave and Stoic

of Epictetus. Epictetus was first and foremost a Stoic, and his writings were remarkably focused on the demands and concerns of living an ethical life within that system.

THINGS IN AND OUT OF OUR CONTROL

The *Handbook* begins by saying we must understand that everything we are involved with in our life, everything we experience, is either in our power or not in our power. We have to not concern ourselves with the things not in our power, such as our reputation or disease, but must instead channel our wisdom and attention on those things in our control, such as choice, desire and opinion. When we realize that many things are not in our power, then we can also say they do not belong to us, they are not in our possession. We have no right to expect that they should always be ours, such as when our property is stolen or when a loved one dies. In our moral imagination, if we have something stolen or lose something of value, we are to consider internally, 'at such a price is tranquillity achieved'. In reorienting our desires we should aim to avoid things contrary to nature, but we should not, indeed, cannot, desire to avoid things that are out of our control such as death or poverty. Not only should we not concern ourselves with things not in our power, such as the admiration of others, but should actively seek to despise them.

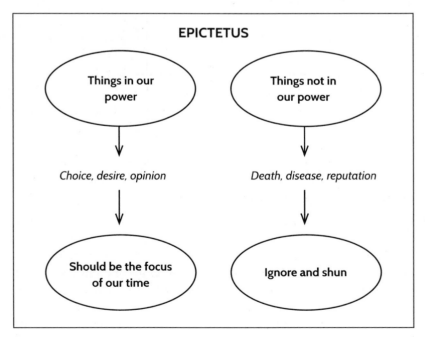

When we consider the things in our lives we ought to take note of their nature. For example, if we know humans are mortal we will not be upset when one of our friends dies, because we know he is human. Similarly, in the case of actions, we should consider beforehand what is likely to unfold. If we go to the market, we should understand that a rude customer may bump our trolley or the bakery may be out of our favourite bread. When it comes to learning of the misfortunes of others, we usually meet this news with some form of, 'Well, this happens'. We should also act this way when we experience our own misfortune.

What?	Knowledge of what vulnerability	Therefore we should not be disturbed when:
Friend	Mortal	The friend dies
Clothing	Moth prone	Our sweater has holes
Car	Flat tyre	We have to buy a new tyre

OUR OPINIONS AND OTHERS' OPINIONS

Epictetus' overarching principle is that events themselves do not disturb us, but rather our thoughts or opinions of those events give us anxiety, fear, pain or loathing. Our opinions shape our perception of an event, but also the opinions of others shape our opinions of events. A striking example of the arbitrary importance we give to others' opinions is that we are as obliged to understand a raven caw, which is a symbol of bad luck, as evil as the death of a loved one. Our perception of both the

The caw of the raven is often seen as a symbol of bad luck

raven and death as something 'bad' is under our control; they do not necessarily mean anything in themselves. The correct attitude then is not to wish for things to turn out as we wish, but for us to wish that things turn out as they actually do turn out to be.

Event	Meaning society gives to it	Actual meaning
Raven cawing	Bad omen	Neither are in our power
Friend dying	Bad omen	To control, we need not be disturbed

Besides being prepared for ill fortune beforehand, by taking stock of and contemplating our daily courses of action, we can also meet it head on by turning it to a good use. If we are tempted to sexual relations with an attractive stranger, this can be a moment for the building up of temperance. When it comes to human relations, it is particularly difficult to remember those things that are not in our power or control. For we often wish to control the behaviour and attitudes of others, when this is not in our control. In the case of insult or offence, it is our opinion of the insult that provokes us, not the insult, so there is no reason to let the insult provoke us. One particularly useful application of this notion is our understanding of death. Instead of being in fear and anxiety about death, we should keep it before our eyes constantly and in this way we will act soberly and rationally in our daily lives.

*For Epictetus, life was like a banquet. It is there to be enjoyed,
but we should not take more than our fair share*

METAPHORS FOR LIFE

Epictetus liked to use metaphors as an explanation for how to live life. In one respect our life is a banquet. We are to joyfully partake of life, but not take more than our share, nor wish for more than can reasonably be ours. Just as at a banquet when we take as much food as propriety and necessity allow, so we should behave in our daily life. Another metaphor is the stage of life. That is, we are to conceive of our life as a play, in which we have no say as to our role. But if we have a large role, that is, a long life, we play that part; if a short life, then we should embrace that life role just as readily. And whether we play the part of a beggar or a nobleman, we should easily accept either of these roles. We should accept things that happen to us which are out of our power, but we should also accept things that happen to others, which are also out of our power. That is, we should not be jealous of the good that befalls others. When we go out into the world as moral actors, it is advisable to imagine what an excellent sage such as Socrates or Zeno would do in each situation.

SELF-ESTIMATION AND REPUTATION

Our own life is to be guided not by the opinions of others, but by what appears best to us. An acceptance of this prepares us for the life of philosophy, which we will be mocked for embarking upon. Paradoxically, however, once we have made progress in our ethical life those same people will admire us. For Epictetus, a large part of seeking the approval of others is tied up with the seeking of external things. The pursuit of these externals surely, he thinks, leads to an unhappy life. One consequence of this idea is that wealth does not make a man good, it only makes him wealthy. Epictetus answers an objection on this topic to the effect that if one is ambitious after fortune, then one can help his friends and country after attaining such a fortune. Epictetus' answer is that if one can attain this fortune in an honourable way, then one should. However, if it involves corrupting oneself in any way, then it is much better to be an honest, good and poor man to his friends and country rather than a dishonest, corrupt and rich man.

THE GODS

Epictetus believes that there are gods and that we should have the right opinions about them. Chief among these is to believe in their existence and to submit to their will. This submission is exemplified by going along with the things that have been allotted to each of our lives. Epictetus promotes divination on the grounds that it shows us what the gods wish for us, so that we can better align our wishes to theirs. The precepts and laws we live by ought to be considered as commands of the gods, and their transgression an act of impiety.

Epictetus supported divination as a way for us to align our wishes with those of the gods

DAILY LIFE

In Epictetus' view we are to live a life characterized by abstention and moderation. With the goal of consistency in mind, we should act with others just as we do when alone. In this we should generally be silent and speak only when necessary. We should refrain from excessive laughter, and the taking of oaths. In all things needed for the body in some way, such as food or clothing, we should make do with the minimum. Besides the practice in moderation this provides, it also rightly subordinates the body to the mind, which is what Epictetus says we really ought to focus on.

In each act, the best way to proceed is to make a full account of the first and last step. If we wish to attain something good, like the achievement of an Olympic athlete, we must consider all the work such as the diet, the exercise and the discipline contributing to success. Only with the totality of a choice in mind can we make a rational decision. This applies to pursuing Olympic success through external things as well, such as money or glory, which will ultimately lead to failure.

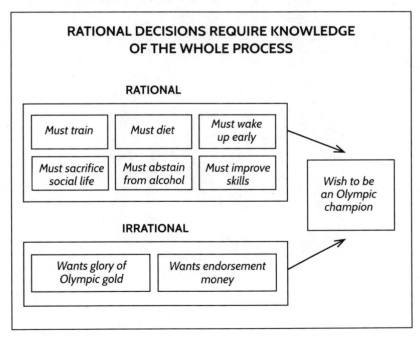

RATIONAL DECISIONS REQUIRE KNOWLEDGE
OF THE WHOLE PROCESS

RATIONAL

Must train
Must diet
Must wake up early

Must sacrifice social life
Must abstain from alcohol
Must improve skills

Wish to be an Olympic champion

IRRATIONAL

Wants glory of Olympic gold
Wants endorsement money

THE END OF THE HANDBOOK

Epictetus ends the *Handbook* by quoting two philosophers. The first is Cleanthes the Stoic, who beseeches Zeus to lead him on the chosen path and, by submitting to this necessity, to become happy and wise. The second philosopher he quotes is Socrates, who reminds us that even the apparent great evil of being killed, because it is not in our power and does not affect our soul, will not harm us.

In the Handbook*, Cleanthes asks Zeus to lead him on the chosen path and thereby make him happy and wise*

Key points

- Epictectus' *Handbook* divides things into those within our power and those not in our power; the former mostly deals with our ethical life, things concerning our desires, hopes, and opinions, and the latter, things like reputation, disease and death.

- Things in themselves do not cause us distress, but rather our mental understanding of these things, therefore when we consider the nature of things, if something happens to them, like death, we are not disturbed.

- Difficult situations should be embraced as opportunities to increase our virtue, such as temperance or patience, and if we always have death on our minds, we will tend to behave better.

- We should be swayed by what we think is good and not by our reputation in others' eyes; in this sense, the pursuit of wealth is permissible if it is done in an honourable way.

- Epictetus believed that the gods should be honoured by submitting to their providence in determining our lives, and that laws are in some way the commands of the gods and, as such, have to be obeyed as part of piety.

- For Epictetus daily life should be characterized by humility and moderation, including an embrace of a meek, consistent personality, whether with company or alone, and by making rational choices.

Chapter 20

Marcus Aurelius

Marcus Aurelius Antoninus was a Stoic philosopher and an emperor of ancient Rome. At the age of six he was enrolled into the order of Roman noblemen and wore the gold ring and tunic denoting this status. His education was liberal enough to include the study of Greek, in which language he wrote the works we have today. At age seven, he became a priest of Mars, involving many archaic ceremonial duties, which he assumed with the necessary gravity. One of these duties was to throw crowns on the couch of Mars. On one such instance, his crown landed

Marcus Aurelius was both philosopher and Roman emperor

directly on the head of the statue of Mars, an occurrence later interpreted as a prophecy of his taking Roman rule.

Marcus' philosophical training began at age 11 when he took up the modest discipline of a philosopher, with its abstemious diet and habit. He became emperor at around age 40 and wrote his work, *The Meditations*, mostly while on campaign against military threats to the empire.

THE MEDITATIONS

The Meditations is the customary title we have given to the philosophical work of Marcus Aurelius, although it is believed this title was bestowed well after his death. As it is, it is not even an accurate rendering of that title. The Greek title is something like *Things for Myself*, an account of thoughts Marcus Aurelius used as a discipline and memoir of his moral thought. The work is divided into 12 chapters, amounting to a little over 100

From his childhood, Marcus Aurelius was a priest of Mars, from which he took an early interest in philosophy

pages in Greek. Besides this conventional literary division, it is difficult to say what, if any, structure the work possesses. Instead of unfolding a line of continually developed thought, *The Meditations* instead express themes. Additionally, a great part of the work consists of aphorisms and occasional anecdotes, all of which serve to demonstrate the text's nature as an aid for the remembrance of ethical improvement. Due to the overwhelmingly aphoristic nature of the work, what follows are illustrative and noteworthy paraphrases of each book from *The Meditations*, rather than a comprehensive (or even partial) summary of the work.

Book 1

In this book Marcus gives thanks to everyone who in some way has contributed to his life. In formulaic dedications he first recognizes from whom he received and then what he received. For instance he says, 'From my father I learned meekness and steadfastness...'. In a similar manner, he thanks all those who have contributed to his upbringing and fortune, focusing on his relatives and teachers, ending with a long thanksgiving to the gods.

Books 2 and 3

Book 2 begins with the acknowledgement that we will meet with unsavoury people today. Nevertheless, these people are as they are because of the ignorance of what is good. We must remember that such people can never harm us. With this view of providence and our role in it, we cannot consider death as evil. Marcus insists that knowledge of oneself is the highest form of knowledge, which includes knowledge of how to peacefully submit to one's role in the universe.

Book 3 admonishes us to keep before us the advancing fate of death, both because of its reality and for the fact that wisdom is so seldom attained before it arrives. All actions are to be undertaken only when guided by right reason in accord

We should not think of death as evil and we must peacefully submit to our role in the universe

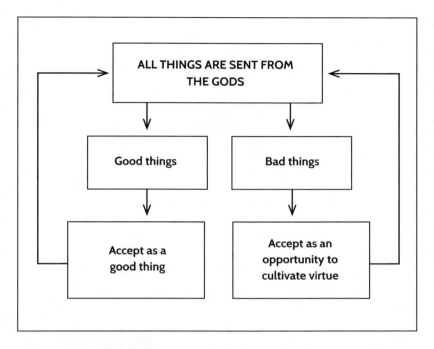

with justice, truth, temperance and fortitude. One way to do this is an accurate inventory of things in our life. We should take account of what each thing is and how it influences our development of virtue; all the time considering that it was sent from the gods for this purpose.

Book 4

Book 4 again attends to the reality of death, emphasizing the brevity and transience of our current way of life, which ought to be subordinated to our reason and nature.

Book 5

Book 5 begins by asking us to consider the feeling we have when we wake up and dread facing our daily task at hand. We are to combat this feeling by considering that we were brought into this universe to do the very work that we are doing. In the middle of this chapter he recites the Stoic belief in an active and passive principle, as well as the eternal dissolution and creation of the universe. Near the end of the book he

'Armpit odour has to smell like the thing it is'

armpit odour

asks whether we are offended and bothered by someone with noxious breath or armpit odour. His reminder to us is that such body parts have to smell like something.

Book 6

In Book 6 we are summoned to remember our place in the providence of the universe. A great exercise for considering the contempt we ought to

Wine comes from nothing more than rotten grapes – remembering this is a form of practising contempt for external things

CULTIVATING CONTEMPT FOR EXTERNAL THINGS

'Prestigious' view	Stoic view
Choice meat	Dead carcass
Wine	Rotten grape
Robe	Spun from a shorn sheep

have towards external things is to remember from where they came. For instance, this 'food' is the dead carcass of an animal, this 'wine' is from a rotten little grape and this 'robe' is from a shorn sheep. Nature is a good model for us to accept our role. The sun does not wish to perform the task of the rain, Marcus points out.

Book 7

Book 7 concerns nature and the benevolence we are to have towards our fellow man. One new idea that emerges is that Marcus advocates embracing 'change'. Without change things cannot conform to the nature of the universe, which is always changing:

Wood becomes fire, reflecting the universe's nature of constant change

wood undergoes change to become fire, food is changed in digestion. Thus we are not to fear or resist change. We are to be compassionate toward the world, for the gods have had to put up with it for eternity, so we, merely wretched creatures within it, should endure it as well.

Book 8

In Book 8 Marcus acknowledges that with his background he cannot claim the upbringing of a philosopher. Moreover, he seems to imply that he longs for that type of validation, but that this seeking after a reputation is vain. He instead refocuses on the effort to cultivate philosophical virtue, goodness and justice, in the context of the distractions of an emperor.

Book 9

Book 9 repeats familiar themes on the impiety of unjust acts, the shunning of vices and vanity, and the acceptance of death. On the latter count, Marcus says we should eagerly await death. Moreover we should anticipate our souls coming out of our bodies in the same way we anticipate a baby coming out of the womb. The gods have even appointed people who are wicked and we should not become angry with these people.

Book 10

Marcus begins Book 10 with the yearning for the perfection of the soul. He is consciously aware of the effect that his politics in Rome and his duties in war will have on the cultivation and obedience of his maxims. The good life is lonely and difficult, such that fellow man shuns you. In

Being separated from each other socially is like a branch broken off a tree

this regard, live as if you were on a mountain, secluded from all and yet visible to all as an example.

Book 11

In Book 11 Marcus praises the soul's ability to contemplate itself. He also enumerates philosophical sayings and anecdotes of others as a tool for ethical development. We are necessarily bound up with each in a social manner, just as a tree has many branches. To be separated from the branch by being broken, is to be separated from the tree. In the middle of the book, he lists ten ways to avoid anger at other people. Among these are the ideas that we have many faults of our own and that we will shortly pass away.

Book 12
The concluding chapter, Book 12, begins by appealing to our happiness, which we may achieve if we do not compare our pasts and we commit our trust in the future to the gods. Marcus speaks of justice, the transience of life and taking things for what they really are in the context of Stoic dogmas such as the active and passive principles of the world and the human being consisting of body, soul, and mind. The end of *The Meditations* likens our lives to those of actors. We ought not to complain about how long we have on the stage of life, but rather be grateful that the same creator who put us on the stage has the authority and good will to remove us as well, for the goodness of the theatre of the world.

■ 10 WAYS TO AVOID ANGER AT OTHER PEOPLE

1. Recognize that all humans are created for the sake of each other.

2. Recognize what kind of character people have.

3. People only act unjustly through ignorance.

4. You have as many vices as others.

5. Some people act as they do because they blindly follow precepts.

6. Remember we all die.

7. Actions don't offend us, it is our opinion of these actions.

8. Our reaction to wrongdoing is worse than the wrongdoing.

9. A kind disposition does more to correct an erring person.

10. It is madness to think a bad person will do no wrong.

Key points

- Marcus' great work, *The Meditations* are intended primarily for his own use as a memoir and gauge for progress. As such the work defies structure; rather, it is a work of themes, thoughts and examples.

- There are 12 books in *The Meditations*: Books 1, 2 and 3 give thanks to people, and are concerned with the role of death, and the insignificance of things outside the realm of the moral.

- Books 4, 5 and 6 stress the transience of life and focus on reason in living, the roles of the lowly and the important in the universe, and not to care too much for external goods.

- Books 7 and 8 exhort us to a compassion for our fellow man and remind us that change is good; Marcus' desire to appear a philosopher is reflected upon as a vain wish, and he instead chooses to follow after a life of virtue.

- Book 9 urges us to make peace with death, focusing instead on virtue, embracing the oncoming spectre of death with joy.

- In Book 10, Marcus yearns for the perfection of virtue, which is constantly impeded by his daily duties as emperor; Book 11 focuses on the many similarities we have with each other and presents a list of how not to be offended.

- Book 12 ends with the goal of happiness, practising the virtues and the providential fit which the gods have ordained for each of our lives, which we must play to the best of our ability.

Chapter 21

Plotinus

Plotinus (*c.*204–270AD) was a philosopher who clearly engaged with Aristotelian and Stoic thought and was thoroughly committed to the Platonic system. Nevertheless, he was a remarkably original thinker. Despite this originality he has a deserved reputation for being obscure partly owing to the choice of his topics, partly to the composition of his work, which his biographer and editor, Porphyry, tells us that owing to poor eyesight he refused to revise once it was written.

Plotinus was an original thinker who owed some of his obscurity to his poor eyesight, which prevented him from revising his work

Born in Egypt, he did not commit himself to any philosophy until the age of 28, when he studied under Ammonius Saccas, a teacher philosophically influenced by Plato. It is due to the work of Porphyry that we have preserved for us the work called the *Enneads*, Plotinus' only work. The

Porphyry was Plotinus' biographer and editor and provides much of our knowledge of the philosopher

name comes from the Greek word for nine, because each of the six books of this work contained nine chapters. As mentioned, Plotinus wrote on incredibly obscure aspects of philosophy, and his writing style is far from lucid, often leading to ambiguities for many readers.

SOUL, BODY AND MATTER

Like Plato, Plotinus believed that humans are composed of body and soul. The body depends on the soul for its existence, but not the soul on the body. The soul, moreover, is present in the body, which invites the question as to how something incorporeal can reside in or be present with a body. Plotinus' answer is that we mistakenly try to understand the soul through ideas about corporeality. There is no difficulty in the soul residing throughout the body, because it is only body that can restrict another body from being in the same place. For example, a boulder can prevent someone standing in the place the boulder takes up, but soul has no such restriction, because it is not body. Even though soul is present in body, it is the latter which is dependent on soul. Soul is that which animates corporeal things, giving them their arrangement as unities and living things. However, for Plotinus soul is fundamentally desire, which seeks to be satisfied in food, drink, sex, sleep and knowledge.

A boulder can prevent the body of a man from being in the same place as the boulder, but not the soul

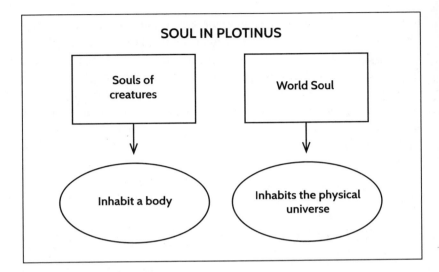

The Soul and World Soul

Along with the individual souls of living things – man, animals and plants – there is also a World Soul. The World Soul animates the visible, physical universe. The workings of this World Soul explain the orderly behaviours of the universe. For Plotinus the soul of animated creatures and the World Soul are the same in kind, although apparently differing in function. The soul is the lowest principle in the three-part metaphysical hierarchy of soul, Intellect and the One.

Body

Let us distinguish between the body of individual living livings, as above, and body more broadly considered as matter, although an animal body in the first sense is certainly still matter in the second sense. In the case of material body, Plotinus believes it is subject to change because it is a composite, formed in one way or another from earth, air, water and fire. As such, it is clearly one level below soul in both worth and importance to Plotinus.

Intellect

The principle above soul is Intellect. As the name Intellect (*nous*) implies, it is something that is actively thinking. What Intellect thinks are the Platonic Forms, unchanging ideals of which things in the earthly, temporal realm are merely copies. Unlike Soul and Intellect, these Forms are not considered principles. They are merely the objects of thought for Intellect, internal to Intellect, where both somehow depend on each other. It can be said that the Intellect and the Forms are one in the activity of thinking. Nevertheless, even though there is a considerable amount of unity within the Intellect and the Forms, there is still difference or multiplicity because there is always minimally: (1) what is thought, and (2) that which does the thinking.

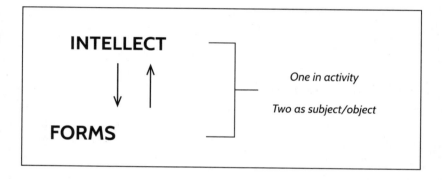

The One or the Good

Above the Soul and the Intellect, the highest principle for Plotinus was the One or the Good. The One is that principle which, in contrast to both the Intellect and Soul, shows the highest degree of unity, a kind of perfect simplicity. The Intellect is less simple than the One because for the Intellect there is a thinker and thoughts, a division into two, and there are furthermore many objects of thought. Thus there is a multiplicity in the Intellect even though it still shows more unity than does Soul. Soul, although completely present throughout a whole body as a unity, is nevertheless present in its relation to body, which is itself composite and divided, both in space and in time, because it is subject to change. So soul has less unity than Intellect, though of course it has more unity than body. So body is the least unified, followed by Soul and then Intellect, while the One is a complete unity.

Since thinking is what explains how the Intellect has less unity than the One, it should be no surprise that the One does not think, and furthermore, cannot be thought. Consequently, the One does not love or hate, perceive or undergo any change to itself. The One is so utterly

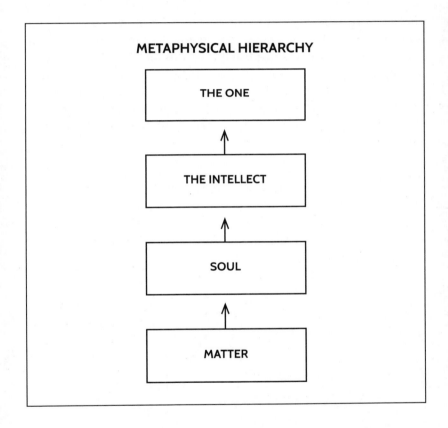

transcendent that it is said to be beyond being. Nevertheless, this does not put it in the realm of Forms, which Intellect thinks. It is beyond being because we cannot say anything about it. As a matter of fact, to posit it as being anything, to say the One is X, is to admit division and multiplicity into the One. The only reason that the One is also called the Good is that, for Plotinus, unity is the same as the good, because to be simple and unitary is to be perfect, without lack or flaw.

'Double Activity' and Emanation

Plotinus believed that everything flows or emanates from the One. In order to understand this emanation we first have to explain the idea of double activity. Double activity is the idea that a cause of something has two activities, one proper or internal to itself, and another causing a change in something else externally. Plotinus uses several metaphors to illustrate this, such as fire, snow and the sun. If we focus on fire, we can say its primary activity is just being what it is, fire, while its secondary activity is producing heat in some other thing.

One aspect of this double activity is that the cause does not undergo change; it stays the same throughout. Here the fire metaphor fails because fire contributes to its own extinguishment. A second and perhaps more important feature of double activity is that the primary activity is

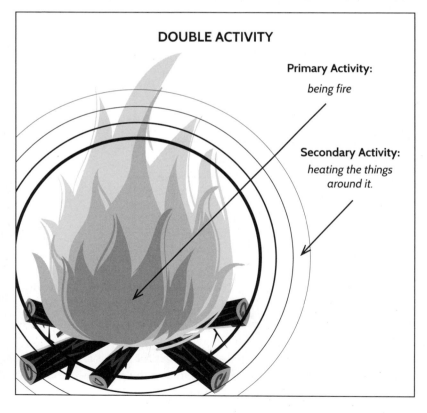

DOUBLE ACTIVITY

Primary Activity:
being fire

Secondary Activity:
heating the things around it.

superior to the secondary. This is well illustrated by the fire metaphor because fire itself is always hotter and fierier than the room it warms. This process of emanation is how Plotinus explains the derivation of Intellect and soul from the One. That is, Intellect is the secondary activity of the One and, in turn, soul is the secondary activity of the Intellect. It is unclear whether Plotinus believed the soul in turn produces matter, though it seems likely. Ultimately though, everything which exists comes to be or emanates from the One.

Two Problems for the One

There are two problems for Plotinus' understanding of the One, which he answers in a philosophically interesting way. The first is that he speaks of the One even though he explicitly says we cannot speak of the One. His answer is that when we speak of the One, we are not actually speaking of it; we are actually saying something about ourselves. That is, when we speak of Intellect, soul and body emanating from the One, we are saying something about those things as effects and not speaking about the One. Plotinus likens this to 'circling around' the One, coming near, backing away, but never actually peering into the actuality of the One.

The other intriguing problem is that the One, also considered the Good because of its simplicity, as the source of everything, must also be considered the source of evil. One answer is that evil is describable as the lack of being which the One, Intellect and the soul possess. In

As we become more closely tied to the material world, our souls fade and we become ignorant of the life of the Intellect and the One

this sense, Plotinus often associates evil directly with matter. If we also consider moral evil, as produced by moral agents such as ourselves, it is caused indirectly by our close relationship with matter. Becoming knitted to a material world and material life, our souls, as it were, are weakened by matter to become ignorant of our higher life in Intellect and the One.

THE ETHICAL LIFE

In the previous sections we have discussed fundamental reality and the principles explaining that reality. Here we turn to Plotinus' conception of how to live one's life. When we conceive of ourselves as humans, we ought to recognize that we are more soul than body. As souls we must remember the ultimate source from which we have descended, the One. Yet our current status as souls dwelling within enmattered bodies drives us to neglect and be forgetful of our ultimate source. Yet, odd as it sounds, part of our soul remains in the world of the Intellect. It is to the Intellect that our soul longs to return, where, in turn, we can be as close to the One as possible. In this sense, the aim of happiness in this world is to seek a likening of ourselves to God, understood as the One.

Key points

- Plotinus, a true acolyte of Plato, believed that the human has both a body and soul, but the body is subordinate to the soul and since the soul is not spatially restricted, as body is, there is no problem with soul residing 'in' a human body.

- The hierarchy of Plotinus descends as follows: the One, Intellect, Soul, and finally matter; the One is a unity more so than Intellect, which in turn is more unified than Soul, which in turn is more unified than matter.

- The Intellect is actively and constantly thinking of Platonic Forms, unchanging ideals and paradigms of earthly things. Nevertheless, because it has an object of thought, Intellect is not as unitary as it could be.

- The One is so transcendent that it cannot act nor be acted upon, nor even be spoken about; it is Good because, for Plotinus, good and unity are the same thing, since unity confers completeness.

- Primary activity refers to the activity of a thing itself, while secondary activity is how it affects other things; in this light the Intellect is the secondary activity of the One, and soul is the secondary activity of the Intellect.

- Evil for Plotinus is closely allied with the notion of matter, and our entanglement in matter; in this world of matter, we have forgotten the One, and we seek our whole lives to return to the Intellect where we can contemplate the One.

Chapter 22

The Legacies of Classical Philosophy

Classical philosophy has had a far-reaching impact on both the cultures in which it matured continuing down to the present day. There are almost too many ways in which to measure and discuss the influence of these philosophers, but we shall go through a handful of them.

PRESOCRATICS

The Presocratic search for an explanation of the material world, the quest for an *arche*, meaning that which causes the world to be what it is and how it is made up, went through various stages. Water, air and fire were all proposed, as well as more exotic variations such as the Indefinite and the pair of Love and Strife. One particularly useful variation was the notion of atoms. Leucippus and his student Democritus were the

FIRE　　　　**AIR**　　　　**WATER**　　　　**EARTH**

The elements water, air and fire were all proposed as arche *that could explain the universe*

first proponents of atomism, which, at its most fundamental, is a theory that discrete units of matter compose the universe. Eventually, this was the germ of the idea that led to the modern conception of atomistic theory. Additionally, the search for an *arche* seems to have survived to the present day in the cosmological quest for a 'theory of everything', a principle of explanation of such simplicity and aesthetic appeal that it alone suffices as a cause of the universe.

SOCRATES

Socrates was remarkably influential even within the world of classical philosophy. He was not merely a token of orthodox Platonism, but influenced Epicureans and Stoics alike, and inspired a sceptical approach among Platonists. In the modern era he has sometimes been likened to Jesus Christ, with whom he shared martyrdom, a group of close followers, an admirable life and – perhaps most remarkably – for not having written a word.

Perhaps as a result of Socrates' aloof philosophical opinions, he also inspired among his disciples philosophers of a decidedly opposite tack than Plato. For

Aristippus founded a sect that presented physical pleasures as the highest form of good

instance, Aristippus, who was the founder of a sect of philosophers committed to the idea that physical pleasures were the highest form of good, and Antisthenes, a sophist who did not entirely shake off his sophistical roots.

PLATO

Plato's academic afterlife is well known. Not only did he inspire a sceptical version of his own philosophy, but a revival, in late antiquity, called neoplatonism, of which Plotinus was the most famous, but certainly not the only, proponent. In addition, Platonism has had a long influence in the Western world in its belief in two worlds, the material and intelligible, as well as its transcendent ideals, whether they be Forms or otherwise. The theologian St Augustine, whom we know was influenced by both Plato and Plotinus, references these authors positively in his work. In a sure sign of how later interpreters transform

St Augustine drew inspiration from the work of Plato and Plotinus

classical philosophy to their own ends, among other things Augustine understood the material/intelligible divide to be one between the carnal/spiritual. Of course, Plato's influence was to extend through the Middle Ages, largely through the transmission of the *Timaeus*, a dialogue which needed considerable Christian reworking in order to align with Christian orthodoxy.

ARISTOTLE

Aristotle's intellectual afterlife is long-lived and far-reaching. Beginning with his death and the continuation of his Lyceum, Aristotle's influence also found expression in Alexander the Great, whom he tutored as a child. This inspiration can be seen in Alexander's collections of flora and fauna, as well as his founding of cities and centres of learning. Among these cities, Alexandria of Egypt was perhaps the greatest, and it is from here that the great Hellenistic scholars performed their work of literary criticism, classification of genres and textual analysis.

The city of Alexandria in Egypt was one of the great centres of learning in the classical world

As a strictly philosophical influence, however, Aristotle was neglected for a couple of centuries after his death. With the turning of the millennium, devoted commentators on Aristotle began to appear, the most notable being Alexander of Aphrodisias (late 2nd to early 3rd century AD), Simplicius (c.490–560AD) and John Philoponus (c.490–570AD). In the Latin west a rich commentary tradition was also established, perhaps most ably by Boethius (c.475–526AD), who also translated Aristotle into Latin and incorporated Aristotelian philosophy into the Christian

Giordano Bruno was burned at the stake for ideas he had derived from Epicurus

tradition. This theological bent followed Aristotelianism in the West for a long time, culminating in the work of Thomas Aquinas (c. 1225–1274) who used the tools of Aristotle's philosophy to both defend and enrich the Catholic faith.

EPICURUS

In ancient Rome an Epicurean school was founded in Rome. The school influenced the Roman poets Virgil, Horace and Lucretius. However, one of the contributing factors to the decline of Epicureanism in antiquity was the Epicureans' reticence to take part in political affairs, a near suicidal attitude for cultural influence in the Roman Empire. As the Christian faith spread, Epicureanism was the target of criticism for advocating a divinity that did not intervene in human affairs, no afterlife and a material soul. Among later influences, Giordano Bruno (1548–1600) and Pierre Gassendi (1592–1655) stand out. Bruno was eventually burned at the stake for a number of ideas thought of as heretical, including the infinity of the universe and other worlds, both ideas adopted from Epicurus. Gassendi wrote critical responses to Rene Descartes and multiple works on Epicureanism. His Christian beliefs formed and modified his Epicurean commitments, for example, the idea that all knowledge comes from the senses, not abstract principles.

CONCLUSION

Any discussion of the legacies of classical philosophy necessarily must be cut short, for philosophy has and will continue to

St Thomas Aquinas used Aristotle's philosophy to defend the Catholic Church

influence society. Many more things could be said about, for instance, the influence of Platonic and Aristotelian physics on the Middle Ages. More generally Aristotle's biological works continue to influence our philosophy of biology, setting the groundwork for the empirical study of nature, speciation among living creatures and many other biological concepts. Contemporary philosophers through to the common person on the street are deeply interested in reviving a form of virtue ethics of the type Aristotle promoted. Wherever there are people, there will be thoughts, and very often these same thoughts occur to philosophers and are incorporated into philosophical systems. This is the shared life we all have, not as philosophers, but as humans.

Glossary

Adiaphora Those actions in Stoic ethics which were considered neither good nor bad, but 'indifferent', that is, without any inherent ethical value.

Apeiron Alternatively, the Indefinite, the Unbounded, or the Boundless, posited as a principle of the universe by Anaximander.

Arche A term used by many different presocratic philosophers referring to their respective candidate to explain the material composition and origin of the world.

Arête Literally 'excellence' in any field, but when restricted to humans often refers to ethical life, so in this sense can be considered 'virtue'.

Ataraxia A mental state in which a type of peace or freedom from care follows as the natural result of the Sceptic's philosophy.

Atomism A philosophic theory of Leucippus and Democritus, and later by Epicureans, which posits the material makeup of the world as consisting of minute, 'uncuttable' bodies.

Cosmic Cycle For Empedocles, an endless process of the universe in which fire, air, earth and water were continuously being joined and separated by the forces of 'Love' and 'Strife'.

Cosmology The creation and/or composition of the universe, and the study of the issues involved with these topics.

Counter-Earth A hypothetical planet, which according to Aristotle the Pythagoreans posited solely to make the nine known planets a more mathematically satisfying ten.

Drachma A unit of coinage in ancient Greece.

Eidola Literally a 'little image'. For Epicurus sight involved seeing these *eidola*, which are faithful representations of whatever object they are of, i.e. little images of apples stream into one's eyes if the object of perception is an apple.

Elenchus Literally 'refutation'. This is the method which Socrates employed to take something one of his followers said and use it against that person as a form of refutation.

Epicurean That school of thought which centred around Epicurus and his philosophy, summed up in the *tetrapharmakon*.

Epoche A 'suspension' of judgement, that is, a mental approach among sceptics which tries to avoid the formation of beliefs.

Eudaimonia Literally 'well daemon-ed', meaning that one's life is fortunate in some sense. This ancient term somewhat corresponds to our notion of happiness, except that it emphasizes the objective components of a blessed life rather than the inner, subjective experience.

Form (*eidos*) In Plato, those incorporeal, eternal, changeless, divine models, after which physical things in this universe are patterned. In Aristotle, either can be considered the definition of something or its fully mature actualization.

Gnomon In Pythagoreanism merely a shape, as a carpenter's square. Elsewhere it refers to a kind of solar time-keeping device, like a sundial.

Hegemonikon Literally, 'the commanding [element]'. For the Stoics, the faculty which did both the thinking and deciding for the soul.

(The) Indefinite See *Apeiron*

Intellect (*nous*) A common Greek word for 'mind'. In Plotinus, that state of being which is below the One, which is always contemplating the Forms.

Koine Greek As compared to the Greek of the classical period, a somewhat simplified dialect following the dispersion of the Greek language after Alexander the Great's conquest.

Logos Literally 'word, account, reason, argument', this word is perhaps the most difficult Greek word, for its meanings defy encapsulation in merely one term.

Mind   See *Nous*

Oikeiosis   Literally 'a becoming one's own'. A Stoic doctrine which can be translated as 'affinity', wherein humans, following their natural instincts, enlarge the scope of their relations until they have achieved a kind of community with the world.

The One   In Plotinus, that from which everything else 'flows' out. It is the source of being and existence for everything else, but is itself beyond being.

Pithanon   The 'probable' or 'credible', used to refer to sense impressions, such as those of sight or hearing. A criterion of belief used by Carneades, an Academic Sceptic, as a concession that a sceptical approach to the needs of daily life was often wanting.

Plenum   Latin for 'full'. In Democritean atomism, one of the two divisions of the universe; that which is filled by atoms.

Presocratics   Refers to any philosopher 'before' Socrates, but this sometimes applies to his contemporaries as well, because Socrates is perceived to have initiated an interest in moral instead of physical investigation.

Protagorean Relativism   A belief that the truth depends on what each person decides for him or herself.

Psyche (soul)   In Greek philosophy, the term has many different understandings. It can mean the principle responsible for life, as in Aristotle, an immortal and godlike aspect, for Plato, and even for Epicureans, be a material substance.

Sayables (*lekta*)   Also known as 'speakables,' these are the meanings of a word, but not either the sounds or the letters themselves, understood as signs on a page.

Sophists   A group of 'wise men' who gained prominence in classical Athens for their claims of being able to educate young men for a fee, as well as for demonstrating their verbal dexterity, sometimes duplicitously.

Stoic A philosophical school begun in Athens known, most famously, for their attempt to eliminate the passions from their mental life and an emphasis on the aspect of volition as our most important moral quality.

Symbola A form of Pythagorean catechism, or question and answer, which also served as passwords for those within this secretive group.

Table of Opposites A list of ten opposed pairs used by some Pythagoreans. However, its exact use is unknown.

Tetractys A Pythagorean triangle meant to show certain harmonious mathematical relations, set out as a triangle consisting of dots, with the base of the triangle consisting of four dots, on top of which are three more lines of dots, each higher one having one less, until the topmost is a single dot.

Tetrapharmakon 'The four-fold remedy'. A summary of Epicurus' doctrine using the first four of his *Principal Doctrines*. We are not to worry about pleasing or being punished by the gods, we ought not fear death, there is a limit to the amount of pleasure we can experience, and lastly that pain is either of limited duration or limited in degree.

The Four Roots For Empedocles, a poetic term he used to describe the elements of physical matter, fire, air, water and earth.

Theory of Perception Any philosophical theory which attempts to explain one or more of the five physical senses.

Unity of Opposites An idea found in Heraclitus that despite the inherent strife apparent in opposites, such as health and disease, there is an order, or unity, imposed by nature in the midst of this opposition.

Void In Democritean atomism, that which is not the plenum filled by atoms, a total vacuity of stuff.

Index

Picture Credits

AKG Images: *65*

Alamy: *146, 152, 163, 164, 214*

David Woodroffe: *24, 28 (bottom), 36, 75, 143*

Getty Images: *28 (top), 48*

Metropolitan Museum of Art: *7 (Bequest of Susan Dwight Bliss, 1966), 18 (Fletcher Fund, 1956), 198 (Rogers Fund, 1914)*

Shutterstock: *6, 14, 15, 19, 23 (x2), 25, 35, 38, 43, 45, 49, 51, 53, 54, 55, 58 (bottom), 59, 60, 64, 68, 69, 70, 71, 76, 80, 81, 82, 91, 95, 99, 102, 112, 114, 116, 117, 118, 123 (x2), 126, 127, 129, 138, 140, 144, 145, 148, 149, 150, 160, 166, 169, 172, 180, 182, 190, 197, 200, 202, 204, 205, 206, 208 (x2), 209, 210-11, 216, 220, 221, 224*

Wellcome Collection: *8, 20, 22, 40, 42, 58 (top), 78, 83, 84, 88, 93, 94 (bottom), 98, 108, 115, 120, 125, 133, 134, 158, 162, 170, 175, 177, 184, 185, 186, 191, 225, 226, 228*